Kris Meeke

Intercontinental Rally Challenge Champion

Simon McBride

Foreword by
Ian Sedgwick

Other great books from Veloce –

Speedpro Series
Successful Low-Cost Rally Car, How to Build a (Young)

Rally Giants Series
Audi Quattro (Robson)
Austin Healey 100-6 & 3000 (Robson)
Fiat 131 Abarth (Robson)
Ford Escort MkI (Robson)
Ford Escort RS Cosworth & World Rally Car (Robson)
Ford Escort RS1800 (Robson)
Lancia Delta 4WD/Integrale (Robson)
Lancia Stratos (Robson)
Mini Cooper/Mini Cooper S (Robson)
Peugeot 205 T16 (Robson)
Saab 96 & V4 (Robson)
Subaru Impreza (Robson)
Toyota Celica GT4 (Robson)

General
Daily Mirror 1970 World Cup Rally 40, The (Robson)
Porsche – The Rally Story (Meredith)
RAC Rally Action! (Gardiner)
Rallye Sport Fords: The Inside Story (Moreton)
Works Rally Mechanic (Moylan)

From Veloce Publishing's new imprints:

Soviet General & field rank officer uniforms: 1955 to 1991 (Streather)
Red & Soviet military & paramilitary services: female uniforms 1941-1991 (Streather)

Hubble & Hattie

Complete Dog Massage Manual, The – Gentle Dog Care (Robertson)
Dinner with Rover (Paton-Ayre)
Dog Games – Stimulating play to entertain your dog and you (Blenski)
Dog Relax – Relaxed dogs, relaxed owners (Pilguj)
Know Your Dog – The guide to a beautiful relationship (Birmelin)
Living with an Older Dog – Gentle Dog Care (Alderton & Hall)
My dog is blind – but lives life to the full! (Horsky)
Smellorama – nose games for dogs (Theby)
Swim to Recovery: The Animal Magic Way (Wong)
Waggy Tails & Wheelchairs (Epp)
Winston ... the dog who changed my life (Klute)
You and Your Border Terrier – The Essential Guide (Alderton)
You and Your Cockapoo – The Essential Guide (Alderton)

www.veloce.co.uk

First published in June 2010 by Veloce Publishing Limited, Veloce House, Parkway Farm Business Park, Middle Farm Way, Poundbury, Dorchester, Dorset, DT1 3AR, England.
Fax 01305 250479/e-mail info@veloce.co.uk/web www.veloce.co.uk or www.velocebooks.com.

ISBN: 978-1-845840-71-6 UPC: 6-36847-04071-0

Readers with ideas for automotive books, or books on other transport or related hobby subjects, are invited to write to the editorial director of Veloce Publishing at the above address.
British Library Cataloguing in Publication Data – A catalogue record for this book is available from the British Library.
Typesetting, design and page make-up all by Veloce Publishing Ltd on Apple Mac. Printed in India by Replika Press.

Kris Meeke

Intercontinental Rally Challenge Champion

Foreword by
Ian Sedgwick

Simon McBride

Contents

Acknowledgements & foreword

Acknowledgements

This is the part of the book that has caused me the most worry. Firstly I apologise if I have left anyone out.

Above all, I would like to thank my family and friends, and Ian Sedgwick for being the best PR in the business and going beyond the call of duty. Thanks to Kris Meeke and Paul Nagle; without them none of this would have been possible.

Many other individuals who I need to thank include: Kevin Jones, Craig Morrow, Andrew Didlick, Christian Stein, Melanie Kent, Jon Goodman, Marc Van Dalen, Gerry McGarrity, Charlie McGuckin, and Rod Grainger at Veloce for having the foresight and for giving me the green light to go ahead with this project. Thanks to Peugeot UK for the majority of images. The author shot all additional material.

Foreword by Ian Sedgwick

2009, what a year. It'll go down in my memory as the year I got to work with two of the nicest guys in rallying, Kris Meeke and Paul Nagle, and share with them a great adventure.

Like all adventures there were ups and downs, but, through it all, there was a realisation that this was the beginning of what I'm sure will be a great career for two future World Champions. This is a story that shows that, even when you think you have to let go of your dreams, an opportunity is just around the corner. Hard work, belief in your abilities, and persistence will pay off, as they did for Kris when circumstances brought us together in 2008. Kris had not had a regular drive since he drove for Citroën in JWRC; I'd been given the responsibility to put Peugeot UK back on the UK rally map. Then a mention of

a name by Marc Van Dalen of Kronos, a meeting in an airport, and the rest is history.

When we turned up in Monte Carlo we were just another car running alongside 2008 IRC Champion Nicolas Vouilloz ... then Kris set the fastest time on the final stage of day one, live on TV. Suddenly everybody was talking about Peugeot UK and Kris Meeke. Unfortunately, this was also the lowest point of our championship when Kris was caught out by the ever-changing conditions and crashed out on the second day.

At the next round in Brazil, however, we won our first IRC rally. I will never forget the agonising wait for Kris at the end of the final stage and the sheer joy and happiness on the faces of Kris and Paul when they crossed the time control as winners. It was a great party that night.

From Brazil we went to the Azores, and even a tropical storm could not stop Kris and Paul. Win number two really made everybody take note of them and the Union Jack-liveried Peugeot UK 207 S2000.

Next, we went to the legendary Ypres rally, where no-one is meant to win on their first visit. In the UK, we had a change of Managing Director; Jon Goodman had joined us from the other side of the service area – he'd been responsible for Peugeot Belgium and Luxembourg, which was running Freddy Loix and Nicolas Vouilloz. I asked him who he thought would win the rally, and he said, "Freddy." I said, "I think Kris can win it!"

Then followed an unbelievable battle between the Ypres master Freddy Loix and Kris, with Kris checking into the final time control the winner, an achievement even more special as his father Sydney was there to witness it; on Father's Day of all days.

5

Next stop was Madeira (a rally Kris and Paul didn't win), then the Barum Rally in Czech Republic where Kris fought back to finish second from a lowly 33rd after a puncture, Spain another second, and then the legendary Sanremo rally.

Going into Sanremo Kris had a one-point advantage over Jan Kopecky, and the game plan was to score as many points as possible. Then on the second stage, Kopecky ran wide, hit a wall and suddenly he was out of the rally.

I stood at the end of the third stage with this book's author, Simon McBride, trying to confirm Kopecky was out. When we got confirmation, we both realised Kris could win the Drivers' title, here in Sanremo. At the end of day one he was fourth and needed to win to take the title. What occurred on day two must be one of the most remarkable drives in any rally championship. Kris was allowed to push as hard as he wanted on the first stage and see if he could take time out of the leaders. It wasn't going to be a matter of 'if,' he destroyed them and won the rally, the title and the recognition his drives this year have earned him.

The other person, without whom this story would not have happened, and about whom you will learn more as you read this book, is Paul Nagle, Kris' co-driver. Paul, like Kris, lives and breathes rallying, and is the real unsung hero of this story.

It's been a pleasure to get to know and work with Kris and Paul, and together share this great adventure, and I'm sure that you'll enjoy the story of our amazing Championship winning year in the 2009 IRC.

Ian Sedgwick
Peugeot UK PR Manager
Responsible for the 2009 IRC Programme

Chapter 1

Alarming!

This is one of the shortest chapters in this book, but it's also probably one of the most important in the story of the Meeke/Peugeot partnership ...

Kris was supposed to take the early flight to Birmingham out of Belfast International for a meeting with Peugeot. But the problem was his alarm clock hadn't gone off, and Kris slumbered on blissfully unaware that his future career was hanging in the balance.

Peugeot UK PR Ian Sedgwick remembers that morning well: "I was there to meet Kris from the airport, and all the passengers came off the flight, I thought he must have luggage, I'll hold on for a bit, but there was no sign. I was getting worried ..."

Ian was right to be worried, but he persevered and, eventually, Kris answered his 'phone. Realising what had happened, Kris promised Ian he would do anything for him as long as he could get the meeting postponed. Ian worked a small miracle, got the meeting put back to the afternoon, Kris made it to the airport, got a fight across to Birmingham and the rest, as they say, is history ... Kris Meeke and Paul Nagle joined the 2009 Peugeot UK team.

Kris Meeke. (Peugeot UK)

Chapter 2

Meeke – the early years

In 2009, the newly-crowned IRC Champion, Kris Meeke, was a PR dream. In the slick marketing world in which we live, Meeke is the kind of person that companies always want to be associated with. He has charm, personality, and seems to be always smiling ... but things weren't always so straightforward ...

The Meeke name has been synonymous with Irish rallying for many years. Father Sydney is recognised as one of the leading motorsport preparation experts in the country, and worked on the majority of cars rallied by the late great Bertie Fisher.

Kris had been around motorsport since he was a young boy, so it was no surprise that he developed a taste for it (despite having failed his driving test at his first attempt). Kris was not really interested in driving; instead, he got his head down and got a degree in Mechanical Engineering at Queen's University Belfast. After successfully completing his degree, Meeke joined Malcolm Wilson's Cumbrian-based M-Sport, the headquarters for the Ford World Rally Team, as a computer-aided designer. Working with M-Sport made Meeke yearn for a competitive drive ...

In 2000, Peugeot ran a competition to find the young rally stars of the future. Kris entered the competition and got through to the finals at Silverstone. He won the contest, and the first prize was some funding to take part in the Peugeot Super 106 Cup in 2001.

The first person to realise Kris' potential, was Bertie Fisher. He went to see 'rally scout' Gerry McGarrity, who had been working with Mark Fisher, Bertie's son, and told him that he had seen real talent in Kris. Bertie Fisher had a plan – he would try to get Meeke a car to go rallying.

Kris was still working at M-Sport in Cumbria and didn't know that plans were afoot for him to get his foot onto the rallying ladder. Unfortunately, on a bleak day for Irish rallying (January 21st 2001), a tragic helicopter crash occurred, Bertie, son Mark, and daughter Emma all died as a result.

Mark Fisher had been following in his father's footsteps as a rally driver, and, just before the sad events of January 21st 2001, had signed a contract to drive for Peugeot UK. Gerry was supposed to run Mark Fisher in the Peugeot Cup in 2001, but that was not to be. After the dust settled, Gerry spoke to Kris to see if he wanted to drive in some sort of rally championship.

The wheels were set in motion when Gerry received a phone call from Kieran McAnallen (of Toughmac fame), a long-time friend and sponsor of Bertie Fisher. Kieran told Gerry that Bertie had said that Kris had something special. With the long-standing friendship between the Fishers and the McAnallens, Kieran decided that he would carry out Bertie's wishes and give Kris an opportunity to show if he had what it took to be a champion.

Before he left for Coventry, Kieran told Gerry to make sure he came back with a car for Kris, and that he would bankroll it.

Bertie's son Mark had a drive for 2001 in the Peugeot Cup championship, but, due to the fatal helicopter tragedy, Gerry had to return the Peugeot rally and recce cars to Peugeot UK in Coventry. When he arrived at Peugeot he had a chat with Mick Lindford (the Peugeot Sport Manager), and said that he needed a rally car for a young guy called Kris Meeke. The first meeting with Lindford went well, so McGarrity chatted to Vic Lee, who ran the Peugeot BTCC team, and said, in no uncertain terms, that he intended to leave with a Peugeot rally car.

Meeke, Nagle, and the 207. (Peugeot UK)

Meeke plays the Colin McRae Dirt 2 Game. (SMcB)

Vic took Gerry for a tour of the garage, whereupon a particular car caught his eye. Vic said that he couldn't have it – it was the 'celebrity' car, people were coming from Finland to drive it, and getting it from Mick Linford would be impossible. However, Gerry McGarrity *did* get the car, and Kieran McAnallen was a happy man. Project Meeke was 'Go!'

Gerry made a quick phone call to Kris Meeke and told him that he'd be driving a Peugeot in the forthcoming season, and that it was thanks to Kieran McAnallen who was backing the drive.

Before the real action got going that year, Gerry was tutoring Garry Jennings, Stuart D'Arcy, Eugene Meegan, and Kris Meeke at the same time. He took the lads and their cars to Bishopscourt race track for some testing. They got three laps each to show him what they could do.

The fastest feet in the 2009 IRC. (SMcB)

Garry Jennings was the quickest, until it was Kris' turn, that is. Gerry said: "Meeke's pace was unreal, he was crazy fast, in fact. Kris was too fast, and that would have to be reigned in if he was going to progress in the sport."

Gerry remembers the problem with Kris: "He wanted to go faster than everyone else, even when he should have been slowing down for square right/left corners. Kris was an eager beaver. You couldn't harness him in."

McGarrity gave Meeke some advice: if he drove smooth and it felt good, then he would be faster than his competition, he was that good, but he had to stop over-driving the car.

Gerry explained, "There is a great example of this when he was rallying in Kent, it was on a military proving ground and he was coming up a tank ramp and his co-driver was yelling at him that it was a triple caution and that a square left was coming. Kris slotted her into fifth gear and the car ended up in a ball on the other side of the tank ramp. I showed him the footage and asked Kris what he was trying to achieve. Kris replied, 'I knew people would be braking so I decided to keep her (the car) at it.' Now and again he would listen, but his head kept jumping out of gear.

"I took Kevin O'Kane, a former Northern Ireland Forestry Champion, out for testing, I had Kris out that day, too, and I wanted to show Kevin how committed you should be when you're on the stages. I put Kevin in with Kris for a wee run. As the Peugeot 106 came back Kris started to slow up, and before the car got stopped Kevin was trying to get out. Kevin said, 'That boy is mental,' but I replied, 'No, he is gifted.'"

Kris took his first real step into the rallying world after winning the Peugeot competition for new rally drivers in 2000.

Frantically playing the Dirt 2 Game. (SMcB)

Who would have thought that nine years later he would be a Peugeot UK works driver and IRC Champion.

Under the tutelage of Gerry and Kieran, the 2001 season was a mixed one, and it was an emotional year, personally, as Kris' mother passed away that year.

Back on the stages, the speed was there from the start for all to see. On the third round of the championship, the Swansea Bay Festival National Rally, Meeke led his class against more established competitors, proving that he had real talent as he was in similar machinery to his rivals and yet had shown them the way home.

At the end of his first full year as a rally driver, Kris was given an unexpected opportunity to drive a 300bhp, four-wheel-drive Subaru Impreza on the Galloway Hills event in Scotland. The faith the backers of this venture had in Kris was proved well founded, as he took his first ever outright victory – not bad for a rookie.

At the end of the season, Kris decided to tell Gerry and Kieran that he wanted his career to go forward in a different direction. Gerry recalls the meeting, "We were gutted that he left us to go to other places to develop, but that's rallying, and we knew Kris would make it if he could get his head right. It is only now that he has all the bits gelled around him that he can truly show his natural talent."

Unknown to Kris, he had plenty of people keeping an eye on his achievements, and in 2002 that a certain former world champion by the name of Colin McRae thought it would be a good idea to mentor Kris. McRae would prove to be very influential in Meeke's early career.

So, at the tender age of 23, Kris stamped his mark on the rallying scene as he racked up three championships in two years with McRae Motorsport. Meeke won the British Junior Rally Championship title in 2002 and 2003, and the British S1600 crown in 2003.

2002 arrived and Kris contested the British Junior Championship in a Ford Puma. In June that year he won his class in the Scottish Rally after a great drive which was overseen by McRae. He also took second in the category on the Jim Clark, his first full Tarmac event. The third position on the final round of the series was enough for Kris to claim the British Junior Rally Championship title in only his second season in the sport, as well as third in the British S1600 series.

McRae was so delighted with his young protégé that the decision was taken that Kris should move up the ladder and graduate to the Junior World Rally Championship the following year, campaigning an Opel Corsa run by Team Palmer. McRae's intention was that the seven-round series, which took the crews from Monte-Carlo to Turkey, Greece, Finland, Italy, Spain, and finally Great Britain, would be great experience if Kris was to progress to a full World Rally Championship programme at some point.

Meeke made an impressive debut in the 2003 Monte Carlo Rallye, setting two second fastest stage times on the final leg, but was hindered by a string of small problems which blighted his finishing place. The programme was a difficult one. There was no doubt that Meeke had the pace, he lay second in Sanremo and on GB, but crashed out of both events. He did compete on the British S1600, though, and took the British title shortly after his disappointment on the Sanremo.

2004 kicked off in spectacular style, Kris claimed his first podium of the year – a third place on the Monte Carlo Rally, a great achievement on one of the most difficult rallies on the championship. Meeke again mixed British rounds with World outings, and proved he was a class act in the Rally of Wales when he took victory in the S1600. However, luck wasn't with him on the JWRC, as he retired in Greece and Turkey with mechanical problems. He bounced back from these disappointments to score a convincing class victory on the Pirelli Rally.

Rally Finland in the JWRC was another blow to Meeke's confidence. He led the JWRC on the fast, challenging stages around Jyvaskyla, before being caught out in the ruts on the exit of a right-hand corner. He ripped off a rear wheel, hit a tree, and rolled into a ditch. That was the end of Rally Finland.

The 'home' round of the campaign was a further disappointment. On Wales Rally GB the expectations were high, but Meeke was plagued by electrical problems. However, he did set seven fastest times and took second place in the JWRC category.

The next round of the Junior World Rally Championship then made its first visit to Sardinia, and everyone was starting from scratch. Yet again Kris' drive was hampered by mechanical and electrical problems, but, to his credit, he clinched seventh place claiming two championship points.

Fed-up with the problems that the Corsa had brought to the party, McRae Motorsport decided that it would be a good idea to change cars and arranged for Kris to drive a Citroën C2 run by Kronos Racing in the JWRC, at the final round of the championship in Catalunya.

With no time for testing Kris put in an impressive display in the C2, he was even challenging for a podium position when the bad luck gremlins reared their heads and he picked up a puncture. Kris eventually finished sixth in Catalunya, and seventh in the championship, this placing and his ten fastest stage times over the season made him the most successful non-factory supported driver in the championship.

In 2005 Kris drove a McRae Motorsport Kronos Racing Citroën C2 in the JWRC. The campaign started at Monte Carlo and Kris drove brilliantly to win one of the most prestigious rallies in the JWRC category. Kris recorded four fastest stage times on the event, with the Citroën C2 being the quickest car over eight of the thirteen stages.

Sardinia was another good rally for Meeke and his team, he finished in third place, regaining the lead of the championship.

Unfortunately, this was were things went wrong, on the Acropolis Rally, he broke the rear left suspension arm and finished third in the JWRC.

Rally Finland was another difficult rally for team Meeke. When leading the rally, the crew was caught out by an incorrect pace note and went off the road. However, thanks to the Super Rally System, Meeke rejoined the rally on the Sunday and made it up to seventh overall, and scored two valuable championship points.

Kris then got a fantastic opportunity to drive a Prodrive Subaru Impreza S10 WRC run by RED World Rally Team on the 2005 Wales Rally GB. He was very impressive, was inside the top eight, and outpaced his mentor Colin McRae at times during the event.

The following year, 2006, was one to forget, with not many opportunities arising.

During 2007, though, Kris gained valuable experience in world rally cars, and also teamed up with Paul Nagle for the first time. The partnership got off to a great start, and they led the Circuit of Ireland until the engine expired.

Paul Nagle. (SMcB)

Meeke on 2008 McRae Stages. (SMcB)

Meeke and Nagle got a deal together to contest the Killarney Rally of the Lakes. They demolished the opposition and won the event by more than two minutes; impressive stuff.

Rally Ireland was the big one of the year, and Kris thought that if he could put on a good show, then ... who knows ...?

The event began with a super special around Stormont and Meeke was third quickest; a great start. However, luck, again, was not with Kris; he struggled with his road position and then slid off the road into a field and out of the rally. A disappointing way to end what could have been a promising rally.

In 2008, because budgets were being tightened as the credit crunch began to impact on the sport, Kris selected events where he thought he could do well. The highlight was Rally Germany, where Kris had a deal to run a Super 1600 Renault Clio. Meeke and Nagle were 'on fire' and led Sebastien Ogier, who had been 'walking' the category all year. Meeke and Nagle were flying, and led Ogier by over two minutes. However, lady luck deserted Meeke yet again, and the Clio succumbed to an electrical fault 2km from the end of the very last stage of the rally. Meeke and Nagle dropped six minutes and were absolutely gutted, but their drive had been noted. Ogier was a rising star, and Meeke had left him in his wake ...

The next big event for Kris was when he went to Scotland to pay homage to his former mentor, the late, great Colin McRae.

The forests in the Perth countryside were the place to be – you can forget the Cork 20, the Trackrod Rally in Yorkshire,

Meeke gets close to this photographer. (SMcB)

or even the F1 in Singapore, as the McRae Forest Stages 2008 was the motorsport event of the year. There were seventy iconic Fords, a Talbot Sunbeam, and a couple of Porsche 911s speeding through the forest tracks. Among the 140 entrants who competed in the event were three former world champions (Hannu Mikkola, Ari Vatanen and Björn Waldegård), Colin's dad Jimmy, and brother Alister, and his protégé Kris Meeke.

Fittingly, the most popular car in the entry list was the Ford Escort, as Colin had always used his MkII escort as a course car.

The Saturday morning stages opened with Colin's protégé Kris Meeke setting a blistering pace in a Ford MkII Escort – Meeke said at the start of SS1: "I'll be trying in typical Colin McRae style as he was my mentor, and I'll be trying to honour him in a flat out manner." The man from Dungannon stayed true to the McRae legend, fastest in the opening two stages, and leading the Elite part of the rally by 15 seconds. Crawford MacKenzie and Alister McRae were tied in second

Ari Vatanen on the 2008 McRae Stages. (SMcB)

Meeke flies through the stages. (SMcB)

place. While Colin's father Jim McRae lay in sixth place after two stages in the Porsche 911.

Stage three was a dramatic one for Meeke. When the Escort arrived into service the car looked like it had got too close to some of the Perthshire scenery. A disappointed Meeke said: "We were on a tricky section of the stage when Gerry, my co-driver and long time sponsor, gave me a caution to stay wide of a rock. I did so and we touched the grass and the car started to squirm and then we caught a tree with the front of the car and that was that. I'm amazed we got it back to service but the car is too badly damaged to continue. The whole engine block has moved so, yep we are out of the rally. It was awesome while it lasted as I have never driven a BDA-engined MkII Ford Escort before – what a brilliant car, hopefully Colin would have been proud of the first two stage times."

The final stages of the day were a repeat of the morning's tests, and it was Alister McRae and Crawford MacKenzie who were the pacesetters. The battle between McRae and McKenzie was halted early, though, as Colin's father, Jimmy crashed off the road, but thankfully he and his co-driver were unhurt.

The rally finished prematurely, and Alister McRae was announced as the worthy winner. With three former world champions, four British champions, three American champions, and six Scottish champions, it really was a blast from the past. The 2008 Colin McRae Stages was a fitting tribute to 1995 World Rally Champion Colin McRae, who tragically lost his life in a helicopter crash.

Jim McRae in a Porsche. (SMcB)

Alister McRae. (SMcB)

The aftermath of the Escort. (SMcB)

Charlie McGuckin, from Microcam, the in-car camera specialist, shares his memories of a youthful Kris: "The first time I met Kris was at Mark Fisher's funeral, the same time Gerry McGarrity met him. I went for a run with him in the 106, and as soon as I sat with Kris I knew he had a special talent. The speed was in him, he was like a racehorse, which you had to try and tame. I was totally delighted for him when he got the Peugeot drive, it was well earned.

"Over the years I have installed all of Kris' in-car cameras. Some of the footage is spectacular, like when he was leading the Ulster Rally in a Citroën C2 and up against WRC machinery. We knew the boy was world class back then."

Meeke down in the dumps. (SMcB)

Meeke thinking about what had happened. (SMcB)

The damage. (SMcB)

Chapter 3

Drive anything with an engine

From the previous chapters, you can see that you're more likely to see Kris Meeke on a rally stage racing against the stopwatch than racing on a track. However, on a cold day in October 2008, Meeke was invited to race the RX150 in a challenge race at the Croft racing circuit near Darlington. The racing had a little edge to it as Ryan Champion, well known for his exploits in Mitsubishi Evolution rally cars, would also be trying his hand in the RX racers.

Meeke goes racing. (SMcB)

Kris Meeke, Ollie O'Donovan, Peter Stodt, Ryan Champion. (SMcB)

Originally, RX Racing had invited Guy Wilks to go head-to-head with Meeke but, for a number of reasons, he was unable to do so, so Ryan Champion was given the nod.

Meeke had never driven the RX150 in a competitive setting, and told bystanders that he was both nervous and excited about racing on a track with a full grid. Meeke, of course, was a natural, and made it to the Super Final.

Champion and Meeke were in confident mood as they entered the Super Final of the RX Racing Winter Series, with everyone keen to see how the unusual RX machines performed. Dungannon ace Kris Meeke took pole position from Ollie O'Donovan, with former Mitsubishi Ralliart Evolution Challenge winner Ryan Champion lined up in third position on the grid. When the race got underway, 2007 MSA British Rallycross champion and former rally driver, Ollie O'Donovan fluffed his start. This left Meeke and Champion out in front and fighting for the race lead. The racing was frenetic, Meeke led with Champion looking for a way around the Dungannon ace.

This wheel-to-wheel battle, lasted for the entire five-lap race, Meeke was just too good, though, and finished in the end with a gap of about two seconds. Champion finished second and Ollie O'Donovan battled back up the field to third place after his trying start.

A delighted Kris Meeke said: "What a brilliant race! There were lots of people around me. It's not normal not hearing a co-driver shouting the pacenotes into my ear. But this is awesome fun. Rallycross has always intrigued me and, while I had very little preconception of what the RX150s would be capable, I can really see the point. The best bit is that everyone is in the same boat, whether you're a big lad or a small lad, the weight is exactly the same. It's a level playing field. The RX150 is like stepping onto a wild horse and trying to tame it. For a start,

A grid lines up. (SMcB)

Meeke starts racing. (SMcB)

Ollie O'Donovan, Ollie's son, Kris Meeke, Ryan Champion. (SMcB)

you have 150bhp to shift 400 kilos, which means a power-to-weight ratio that's over 500bhp, and it's all going through the rear wheels, via a sequential shift gearbox. I love it! They're just incredible machines to drive.

"They give you a complete buzz, and this championship is fantastic. Now you can race them, hillclimb, or even sprint them. They're brilliant pieces of kit. It was fantastic to win but the buzz of racing these machines is just incredible. We were coming down the start-finish straight at about 110mph, and then you just tip it into the first corner. The buzz is remarkable." I asked Kris if he planned to return the following year, and the Ulsterman replied with a huge grin, "Back next week, you mean!"

Ryan Champion echoed his rival's feelings and thoughts in stating: "That was utterly fantastic, there were some places where I was closing-in on Kris, and other parts of the circuit where he would pull away from me. The RX150s are so equal, and the power-to-weight ratio is phenomenal. I'd love to take part in more of the RX series next year and maybe, next time, I'd take a race win."

Kris runs from cover ... (SMcB)

... and gets sprayed with champagne. (SMcB)

Kris and Ollie laughing. (SMcB)

Drying out on the podium. (SMcB)

RX-150, the front. (SMcB)

RX150 technical specification:

Engine – Honda 954cc, 4cyl, 150bhp

Gearbox – 6-speed sequential

Transmission – Quaife gear-driven link drive, automatic torque-biasing differential

Chassis – 1.5in CDS tube, powder-coated. Tested beyond FIA safety standards

Safety – Front and rear bumpers, side nerf bars, integrated fire extinguisher, side nets, rain, light and windscreen wash/wipe system

Brakes – Stainless steel cross-drilled discs all round, with Brembo calipers and bias adjustment

Dimensions:

Length – 2800mm

Width – 1850mm

Weight – 1450mm

Performance: 0-60mph in 3.5secs, top speed 120mph

Weight – 525kg

(All vehicles will be weighted to a minimum of 525kg including driver)

The RX-150. (SMcB)

A few months after his debut in the RX150, Kris would become a works driver for Peugeot UK in the 2009 IRC season – he had got his big chance.

Chapter 4

Paul Nagle – 'Bought a rally car in my school uniform'

P aul began his rallying career in 1998, as co-driver for one of his mates. "Me and my mate went off one day to buy an Opel Corsa rally car, and we were still in our school uniform when we picked up the car. It was a great feeling." A couple of weeks later the pair were dropping off sandwiches to the marshals on a local event. Neither had a competition licence so, unfortunately, they couldn't compete, but they already had 'the bug.' So, that's where it all started for Paul.

From there it went to sitting in with the likes of Eugene Donnelly in the Irish Tarmac and gravel championships. Paul won the Peugeot 206 championship with Garry Jennings; he also co-drove for Rory Galligan and Gareth MacHale.

Things got serious for Paul in 2005/06 when he went to the World Rally Championship in an M-Sport Focus with Gareth MacHale, and did nine or ten rounds of the world championship that year.

It wasn't until 2007, though, that Paul met Kris. Paul said: "We were both at a local rally and we just got chatting. The next time I heard from Kris was when he was stuck for a co-driver in March 2007 for the Circuit of Ireland. We had a problem on the Circuit, the engine expired when we were leading, but we both enjoyed it and knew we could work with each other again."

Paul was still with Gareth MacHale at the time, but then the pair had a massive accident in Sardinia, falling over 100 feet down a valley; the Kerry man claims it was the scariest moment of his life, but thankfully they both walked away from it.

Paul admitted that the accident, because it was so huge, had knocked his confidence. Up to that point rallying had been everything to Paul. He said: "Rallying was my life up to then, but I took a huge step back from it. All of a sudden I didn't want to

Paul Nagle. (Peugeot UK)

go back to rallying, I was comfortable back home in my own environment, and then all of a sudden Kris got the Pirelli drive for the Circuit and told me, you have to go, you just have to come with me. I hadn't been back rallying since that accident in Sardinia, but we went up and we won the rally.

"It spiralled from there, we entered Rally Ireland, obviously we had problems there, we had the pressure. The whole thing was wrong, Rally Ireland at that time was wrong for us, it was great to be there and to be leading, but the pressure was intense, and then we went off. It was a left over a jump into a square right, it was unlucky and sure Eamonn Boland went off at the same place. It was one of those things, just a mistake. Then we had nothing for about a year, we did the odd rally here and an odd one there."

Paul smiled, the Kerry lilt coming across strongly: "I was pushing Kris to do my home rally, Killarney, in 2008. We couldn't get a deal together, which was unreal, as Kris had won the rally in 2007. But we didn't give up, and the week before the rally we got a deal to drive a Renault Clio. We were setting fastest times in a Clio against WRC machinery. We got a slow puncture and we didn't even know it, and we were not carrying a spare wheel because we were traveling as light as possible and that was that.

"The year was a bit hit and miss. Germany was a real turning point, Sebastien Ogier was an up and coming superstar and we went out there and we were in a league of our own. Ogier could not look at our times. We had a technical problem 2km from the last stage, a wire had come loose and we didn't know, it was just one of these things. We dropped six minutes or something and it was disappointing but we had left our mark.

"I got a phone call after the McRae stages last year. It was Kris, and he asked me what are you up to next year? There might be something happening next year? How are you fixed he kept asking."

At that time Paul was co-driving with Barry Clark in his Focus and they were competing on a few rounds of the WRC.

But Paul continued: "Kris kept in touch and told me that this Peugeot UK thing might come off, sure we might have a drive, he just said you just don't know, it is a maybe. The next thing I knew was that we were sitting at the dealer conference over in Birmingham as part of the Peugeot UK team. From then it has been a rollercoaster."

Happy-go-lucky. (Peugeot UK)

Chapter 5
The Intercontinental Rally Challenge

The Intercontinental Rally Challenge (IRC) is a rallying series organised by SRW Ltd and sanctioned by the FIA. The tag-line is: New Rally. New Generation. According to the people responsible, the championship attempts to "give new opportunities to young or amateur rally drivers competing in recognized regional and international rallies, while offering organisers an innovative TV format concept, created by Eurosport."

The championship focuses on Group N (or what is known as the showroom category) and Group A spec cars up to 2000cc (including vehicles that come under S2000, R2 and R3 homologations).

The series was born in 2006 with the name International Rally Challenge, switching in 2007 to its current name.

Kris enthused when talking about the series: "The IRC is a breath of fresh air to world rallying. With the FIA making the decision that the WRC is going Super 2000 in 2010/2011, I couldn't be in a better place. Eurosport is giving the IRC lots of exposure, and I am really happy to be a part of it."

Kris Meeke on the IRC. (Peugeot UK)

Meeke with the S2000. (Peugeot UK)

Champions

Year	Driver	Co-driver	Car
2006	Giandomenico Basso	Mitia Dotta	Fiat Punto Abarth S2000
2007	Enrique García-Ojeda	Jordi Barrabés	Peugeot 207 S2000
2008	Nicolas Vouilloz	Nicolas Klinger	Peugeot 207 S2000
2009	Kris Meeke	Paul Nagle	Peugeot 207 S2000

Chapter 6

Gambling in a credit crunch

The very best have always taken calculated gambles to 'push on.' However, to start a rallying project in the middle of a credit crunch was a ballsy approach to business. As Honda pulled out of F1 and Subaru out of the WRC, Peugeot UK announced it would run Kris Meeke and Paul Nagle in the Intercontinental Rally Challenge – certainly a different approach in a climate when car makers were playing their cards close to their chests.

Peugeot UK must be applauded, not just for signing Meeke and Nagle, but for having the foresight to develop such a programme with Peugeot Sport and Kronos Racing. The Lion-badged cars made the IRC stand out, and it has given us another 'home grown' rally champion to be proud of.

Ian Sedgwick tells the story: "To go rallying was a huge gamble, but our marketing director wanted to put the buzz back into motorsport. Christian Stein had been the man behind the Peugeot Belgium rallying success story and he wanted the UK to have a slice of that cake.

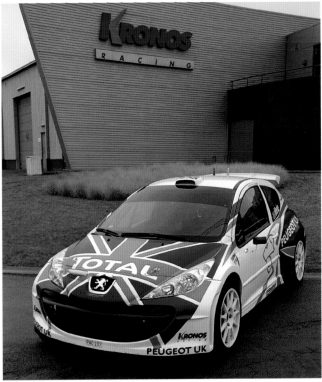

At the 2008 Autosport *Show. (SMcB)*

The 207 S2000 outside Kronos Racing. (Peugeot UK)

The Peugeot 207 S2000 that Meeke would drive on the IRC. (Peugeot UK)

The rear of the 207 S2000. (Peugeot UK)

More of the 207 from the 2008 Autosport *Show. (SMcB)*

"We put our heads above the parapet, just when other makers were diving for cover and withdrawing from motorsport activities. The one point we made is that if we were to do it right, then we would work with the correct people and get, hopefully, a really strong package together.

"We wanted a top line British driver, and Kronos boss Marc Van Dalen told us that we wanted Kris Meeke as our driver. We knew Kris was very quick, and Marc saw that he had real talent, but, more importantly, he had to be a good ambassador for Peugeot, and when we met Kris for the first time in Birmingham airport we knew we had the right man for the job.

"Some dissenters were wary, and told us that Meeke had a reputation, but Marc Van Dalen believed in him and we believed in both Kris and Marc. We told Kris that he had a whole championship and that a couple of podiums and maybe one win would be a great year. He did not have to win or bin, he had a whole campaign to prove himself.

"For me personally Monte Carlo was one of the lowest points of my career, I felt suicidal, we all felt so low, but Kris learnt a valuable lesson that day, as he was told in no uncertain terms, that he could not go through the season binning cars.

Monte Carlo was a real low point, and then we had the 13 hours to Brazil, that was a long flight – we all had a lot of time to think about what had happened at the previous event.

"After the low of Monte Carlo, Brazil was a major turning point in Meeke's career, it showed that he could keep his head and win when the pressure was on him.

"Ypres was an iconic event, Meeke showed his talent, it is such a Tarmac specialist event. To win in Ypres was unbelievable, to me, Belgium was the real pinnacle, in our minds we can win the championship I thought.

"Meeke also proved that he had other dimensions, on a promotional sense, Meeke fronted TV ads and print ads and has become something of a celebrity.

"To get the rallying budget through, using Kris as a promotional tool was always part of the plan, we had to use advertising, and if we made Meeke high then we could make the Peugeot brand high. Rallying pays for itself, the strength of the genre is that it uses cars that you see on the street. It is accessible for all and you can easily go and chat to the drivers, unlike F1. It is a great way to show what the Peugeot brand can do."

Chapter 7
An early Christmas present

Kris Meeke got a brilliant early Christmas present as Peugeot UK was to team up with Kronos Racing to prepare and support a Peugeot 207 S2000, driven by Kris Meeke and Paul Nagle, in the 2009 Intercontinental Rally Challenge (IRC).

The IRC Challenge was to be contested over 12 rounds, starting with the legendary Monte Carlo Rally in January, and finishing in November with the RAC MSA Rally of Scotland.

Kris Meeke was overjoyed at driving a Peugeot in the IRC and teaming up with Kronos, for whom he had previously driven in the Junior World Rally Championship in 2005.

Kris, a previous winner of the British Super 1600 and British Junior Championship, was to be co-driven by Paul Nagle.

There was going to be an element of pressure on Kris and Paul as the 207 S2000 was a proven winner – it had already become the car to beat in the IRC Challenge, and had secured the Manufacturers' and Drivers' Championship, in both 2007 and 2008.

Kris felt like he had won the lottery, it was a dream drive: "Awesome, it has been a lot of hard work and a lot of meetings, blood, sweat and tears to get to here but, as I say, this is just awesome. To be getting a factory drive in the current climate is brilliant, I have to very thankful that things have worked out. It is easy to say now, never give up, but you know, it *is* true. I am just fortunate that I have come across a company that is looking to go the same direction as I am.

Kris Meeke looking forward to Monte Carlo and the start of the IRC. (Peugeot UK)

"Rally Germany and leading Sebastien Ogier proved that I could compete at the very top level. For sure, it really is about not giving up, I have to be so thankful for all my sponsors who stuck with me and had faith in my ability; we singled out events throughout last year and Germany was probably the big one that really caught everyone's attention. I met Kronos in Rally Russia when I was using the Clio. So way back in May we were starting to think about this year, little did I know then, that it would come, in a factory drive with Peugeot. That's the avenue we decided to go down and it has proved to be the right one.

"I had some experience of the PSA group before with the C2, and I have tested the C4 previously. Together with driving the 207 I also have a testing contract with Citroën as well and, with Olivier Quesnel being the boss of Peugeot Sport and Citroën Sport, I couldn't ask to be in a better position. I have to be grateful for it and I have to work hard to make the most of it. This is only the start of the journey, you only get out what you put in. This deal is fantastic but you cannot think you have landed on your feet, I just have to work hard and make the most of it.

"The great thing is that I don't have to prove myself, I have a full championship to think about. Before, I got caught in the trap of trying to prove myself and thought that nobody was looking, and I tripped over myself more times than enough. I have to consider my two teammates (Peugeot Belgium); they finished 1-2 in the championship last year. The Peugeot is the championship-winning car so

Kris is very happy with the testing session. (Peugeot UK)

Meeke and Nagle preparing for the challenge of the Monte Carlo Rally. (Peugeot UK)

I have the best package behind me, but these guys have been driving the cars for two years and I have not even driven it yet. We have got to err on the side of caution with the first event, Monte Carlo, due to the nature of the event, if I want to come away with any points from there I have to be good."

Kris thanked Paul Nagle for his hard work prior to the Peugeot contract: "It is brilliant to team up with Paul. Paul has been awesome when times have been tough, and he has stuck by me through the last few years. I rate him as one of the best co-drivers I have ever had, and for him it is a big opportunity. We both have to knuckle down and make the most of it.

"It is great to have the final event in Scotland and it should be great for Peugeot UK. I just hope to be in a position where I am fighting for the championship on the final round, Scotland has some of the best gravel stages in the world, so it should be a brilliant end of the year. This is an incredible opportunity for both myself and my co-driver Paul Nagle! It brings my career somewhat full circle, as my first introduction to rallying was through a Peugeot UK supported competition in 2000. Some awesome and diverse challenges lie ahead in the 2009 IRC, but we can rest assured that with the support and championship-winning pedigree of both Peugeot and Kronos, we will have the best opportunity to prove our abilities in the coming season!"

An enthusiastic Pierre Louis Colin (Managing Director Peugeot UK) stated: "I am very pleased we have been able to enter next year's IRC Championship with Kris. Rallying is in the blood of Peugeot and it is a good demonstration of the dynamism of Peugeot cars, especially the 207. We know we have a winning car, and in Kris and Paul we also have a winning team. In these difficult times, it is important that you make sound commercial decisions but it is also important to communicate to your customers in a positive way your brand and your commitment to it."

Chapter 8
Be seated

Monte Carlo is the jewel in the crown of world motorsport, and it was to be the principality that would kick off the 2009 Intercontinental Rally Challenge series. Kris Meeke, Paul Nagle, Kronos, and Peugeot UK would start the rally eager for the season to begin and, more importantly, try to kick off the campaign with a good result.

Peugeot UK and Kris Meeke lined up at the start of the 77th Monte Carlo rally, one of the oldest races of its kind, alongside reigning IRC Champion Nicolas Vouilloz and his other Kronos-supported teammate Freddy Loix.

Kris Meeke testing the 207 S2000 prior to the Monte Carlo Rally. (Peugeot UK)

Driving the Peugeot UK Kronos-prepared 207 S2000, Kris had the aim of repeating his previous victory at Monte Carlo back in 2005 in the JWRC. But the pre-rally plans were in danger of coming apart. Kris and Paul were ready to test the Peugeot 207 S2000, but there were no seats; both prefer the Recaro wraparound. Fortunately, though, Peugeot UK PR man Ian Sedgwick went to the Recaro factory in the UK, picked up the rally seats for Kris and Paul, and made his way to Heathrow for a flight to Monte Carlo. Ian laughed: "You should have seen the faces of the passengers when I had to get on the car park bus at the airport with two race seats; probably some of the most unusual hand luggage I'll ever be in charge of on a plane."

After the flight Ian thought it would be a simple job to get the rally seats to the rest of the team as he'd booked a medium-sized car from the airport hire company. However, when he got to the desk, he found to his dismay that the hire company had arranged a Citroën C3 for him, with no sat-nav; not brilliant when you need to transport two race seats to the team and get them there in one piece.

After an adventurous trip, Ian arrived at the test session with the seats in pristine condition. Asked whether he'd had a good trip Ian replied: "I am glad it's over, let's get the seats in and get started."

So, Kris Meeke and Paul Nagle were finally able to get into the cockpit of their Peugeot UK 207 S2000 for a two-day test on closed roads, in preparation for the 77th Monte Carlo rally. Meeke was joined on the test by Sebastian Ogier driving the Kronos Racing-run BF Goodrich Drivers' team car.

The rally commenced in front of the Casino on the evening

of Tuesday 20th January, and finished back in the principality on Saturday 24th. The rally was contested over three legs and included four night stages, with two runs over the famous Col de Turini.

One issue that all the competitors had to get used to were the special studded tyres designed to cut through the ice and snow in order to find grip. With the conditions likely to be very varied, selecting the correct tyre choice could make the difference between winning and losing ...

The all-important race seats wrapped up and in the rental car.

Sideways action from Kris Meeke on his pre-Monte Carlo Rally test. (Peugeot UK)

Meeke and Nagle fly in testing. (Peugeot UK)

Chapter 9

Monte – a lesson learnt

Rallye Automobile Monte Carlo
21-24 January 2009
IRC Round: 1

With Monte Carlo in the fullness of winter, the first round of the 2009 IRC series was set to be a cracker. Kris Meeke had claimed that this rally would be his toughest test yet, and said the 2009 season could be the most important year of his career. The 29-year-old Dungannon ace was in great form in the run-up, and was looking forward to an event he had won in the past at JWRC level.

Kris said: "This is an incredible event. On the recce, we drove each stage three times, and did 4500 kilometres – amazing. And that's before the rally had even started. There's no doubt

Meeke and Nagle battle. (Peugeot UK)

that this is going to be a classic Monte Carlo and a fantastic start to the IRC season."

Kris was certainly revved up for the first round of the IRC: "It's fantastic to start our campaign with Peugeot Sport with the incredible backdrop of Monte Carlo! I've competed on the rally three times before, but the nature of this event, with the unpredictable snow and ice through the mountain passes, always creates a daring challenge!"

Heavy snowfall in the mountains high above the Mediterranean coastline made the tyre selection the stuff of nightmares, however.

Meeke added: "On Thursday, we do two loops of three stages. One of those stages has 40 per cent snow, one of them has loads of ice, and one of them is pretty much dry. How do you pick the right tyre for that? That's what's so fantastic about this event, it's the unknown.

"For me, there's no doubt this is the biggest and most important event of my career. Right now, I wouldn't be anywhere else in the world. I'm so excited about this rally."

Pierre Louis Colin (Managing Director – Peugeot UK) reiterated Meeke's enthusiasm: "Monte Carlo is a great place for the team to start its IRC Challenge. It's a rally which both Kris and Paul know very well, and we hope to give the British fans something to cheer about. It is going to be a fascinating three days and I am sure everybody in the UK will be rooting for Kris."

The 207 S2000 was based on Peugeot's road-going 207, and it had already demonstrated that the inherent strengths of the road car were a perfect foundation to create a class leading rally car.

Meeke and Nagle prepare for the stages. (Peugeot UK)

A number of well-known drivers were there at the start of the rally, including former World Rally Champion Didier Auriol. Three-times winner of the Monte Carlo Rally, driving another Peugeot 207 S2000, Toni Gardemeister, lined up in an Abarth Grande Punto, and Le Mans Peugeot 908 HDi FAP driver, Stephane Sarrazin, drove a Peugeot 207 S2000 for Peugeot Sport.

Conditions were just right for a Monte Carlo rally – snow and ice, and plenty of it. It was set to be a cracker to open the 2009 series.

Special Stage (SS) 1 saw a return to form for reigning champion Nicolas Vouilloz as he set the pace in his Peugeot 207 S2000, 2.9 seconds quicker than the Skoda Fabia of Juho Hanninen, while Finn Toni Gardemeister lay in third, 16.3 seconds

adrift of the leader. Kris was 55.8 seconds off the lead and in seventh overall – a tentative but professional start.

Getting to the finish of the stage was no mean feat, as experienced competitors, such as Luca Rossetti and 1994 world champion Didier Auriol, were among a number of competitors who retired due to the slippery conditions.

After the first stage of the Monte Carlo event, an excited Kris said: "Absolutely incredible, standing in the harbour this morning, some people are going out on studded tyres, some are going out on winter tyres with no studs, some on rain tyres and some on slick tyres.

"The information I had was with the second stage starting in four hours time it was going to be bone dry, hopefully, we went on a slick tyre, I have to say we took a gamble and hopefully it

Meeke and Nagle battle on the snowy alpine roads. (Peugeot UK)

is going to pay off now. It is absolutely incredible conditions, full ice on slick tyres, incredible."

The second stage of the rally saw Stéphane Sarrazin set the fastest time of 14m 28.2 seconds for the 23.27km stage. While, Kris again posted the seventh fastest time, just behind Freddy Loix, but this time he was quicker than reigning IRC Champion and Kronos teammate, Nicolas Vouilloz. Surely, a good omen for the rest of the rally?

As stage three drew to its conclusion it was Kris Meeke who topped the stage time. The St Jean en Royans-Col de Gaudissart 30.39km was electric for Meeke. With a stage win in the bag the confidence was really starting to show.

Kris smiled: "Very surprised with my time on SS3, knew I had a good run, and it was so enjoyable to drive, it was fantastic to get my first fastest time and to get it on snow was mega."

With the first leg completed, Kris was handily placed for the second leg in sixth position overall, 1m 01.3 seconds behind the leader, Juho Hanninen in the Skoda Fabia S2000.

Peugeot Kronos Team boss Marc Van Dalen after day one said: "I am very pleased, the cars are currently 3, 4, 5, 6. It is

Meeke seems relaxed; mechanics work in the background. (Peugeot UK)

Ever-changing weather: dry this time. (Peugeot UK)

not easy regarding tyre choice, and the weather conditions are changing all the time, but the car is there, the drivers are perfect. The team are doing a great job, so far so good. I'm confident."

Being in the points at the end of your first day's competition in a highly competitive series is no mean feat, but Kris showed that, when everything clicks into place, he has the pace to top the timesheets. For the next stage, Kris was hoping that the snow would come.

Kris explained: "On stage three we were down at the bottom of the mountain and I looked up and said that the clouds looks so white up there it must be going to snow, so we gambled on taking studded tyres. It turned out to be an awesome gamble and we got the fastest time. By the time we got up the hill, it was full snow, it had settled on the road, it was deep and streaming past the windscreen. Believe it or not that was the first time I've ever driven a rally car on snow – and now I love it. This car is just brilliant to drive on the white stuff. In fact I hope all the stages today have snow on them. It might be so, according to the weather reports."

On the first stage of the second leg Meeke was again very quick, but it was Juho Hanninen in the Skoda who topped the

Kris and Paul roar through the stages. (Peugeot UK)

times and won the stage. Second placed Stephane Sarrazin went off the road and lost about five minutes, promoting Kris to second overall. Reigning Junior World Rally Champion Sebastien Ogier was now up to third. Things were getting interesting.

Hanninen was certainly in the groove as the Finn set another fastest time on the fifth test, the famous St Bonnet le Froid stage. More than a minute behind, Meeke remained in second overall, with Ogier just over half a second behind the Peugeot UK driver.

A happy Kris at the end of day one. (Peugeot UK)

Skoda was starting to turn the screw on the Monte Carlo rally, however, and Jan Kopecky now set the quickest time on stage six, moving up to ninth overall. Kopecky's teammate Hanninen continued to lead the rally, but there was drama on stage six for Meeke.

Kris had slid off the road in tricky conditions, but fortunately he was able to continue and, by the end of the stage, found himself demoted to fourth overall. Ogier took full advantage of Kris' problems and went more than half a minute ahead and up to second in the overall classification. Peugeot Belgium's Freddy Loix was promoted to third as a result of Meeke's small off.

Stage seven saw another fastest time for Peugeot driver Stephane Sarrazin – the Frenchman was 10 seconds quicker than Sebastien Ogier – but the big news was the retirement of reigning IRC Champion Nicolas Vouilloz. The Peugeot driver had a big off and the impact broke a steering arm, putting him

out of the rally. A disastrous start to his title defence. However, the top four in the overall classification remained the same.

Stage eight would be a warning for the rest of the season. The Skoda Fabia S2000 looked as if it would be a real threat in 2009 as its drivers took a one-two on SS8.

Juho Hanninen won the stage from his teammate Jan Kopecky, this further increased the Finn's rally lead to over a minute and a half from Sebastien Ogier, who remained in second place. Peugeot Belgium's Freddy Loix was third on the stage and consolidated his third place overall. Kris Meeke was still in fourth, poised to pick up the pieces and maybe grab a podium if anyone made a mistake.

Stage nine would change the face of the rally, though, as leader Juho Hanninen dropped down the order with a puncture. Hanninen was five kilometres into the test when he picked up a puncture. The decision was taken to carry on for the remaining 15km rather than stopping, getting out, and changing it.

Unfortunately for the Finn, he lost two minutes to his rivals and this dropped him from first to third overall. This meant that Ogier now led the rally in the BF Goodrich Drivers' Team car by 30 seconds from Freddy Loix. Hanninen was only five seconds ahead of Meeke and Nagle. Peugeot UK could now challenge for a podium position on the final day of the Monte Carlo rally.

On reflection, stage ten will probably turn out to be one of the most important turning points in Kris Meeke's career as a rally driver. It may not have felt like that at the time, when Kris and Paul crashed their Peugeot UK car out of the rally ... but the Peugeot pair were in good company, as Hanninen crashed out on the same stage.

As the news came through on the radio, the Peugeot UK team had been heading into the stage to see their charges through it. They were devastated.

With the drama on SS10, the rally then fell into place for Sebastien Ogier, as the Frenchman went on to a comfortable win in the BF Goodrich Team Drivers' car.

Rallye Automobile Monte Carlo results – IRC

1	Ogier/Ingrassia	Peugeot 207 S2000	4h40m45.7s
2	Loix/Smets	Peugeot 207 S2000	+1m43.6s
3	Sarrazin/Renucci	Peugeot 207 S2000	+2m21.6s
4	Kopecky/Stary	Skoda Fabia S2000	+3m17.3s
5	Basso/Dotta	Abarth Grande Punto S2000	+4m28.0s
6	Romeyer/Fournel	Mitsubishi Lancer Evo 9	+20m30.3s
7	Burri/Gordon	Abarth Grande Punto S2000	+21m23.0s
8	Artru/Virieux	Mitsubishi Lancer Evo 9	+25m50.7s
9	Cavallini/Zanella	Peugeot 207 S2000	+28m44.2s
10	Knapick/Moura	Mitsubishi Lancer Evo 9	+38m32.7s

Meeke and Nagle at full tilt. (Peugeot UK)

Sideways stuff for Meeke and Nagle on the snow. (Peugeot UK)

The Kronos team – drivers and co-drivers. (Peugeot UK)

Nagle's notes

Paul Nagle takes us through Monte Carlo: "It was a whole new challenge, the recce was very difficult, yeah, and the seats came by airmail with Ian Sedgwick, as we prefer the wraparound Recaro seats. It was all very last minute, we saw the car three days before the rally. The recce was very intense, everything was thrown at us, there was snow, ice and rain.

"We had a day-and-a-half testing up in the mountains before the rally started, there was snow and ice and we tried studded tyres for the first time ever, then we tried gravel tyres on snow, we tried dry tyres on snow, we just about tried absolutely everything. The first morning our rivals were going out on all sorts of tyres and we chose slicks, which was a massive gamble. Rewind the clock and we wouldn't have done it as we dropped fifty seconds to the top boys. Stage two was bone dry but we caught a rival and dropped time. Kris wasn't happy as we were fifty seconds off the pace but on the third test we chalked up our first fastest time.

"Leg 2 was another tough day, our gravel crew which you are allowed on the Monte did an awesome job. You know who you are boys! The tyre choice was crazy through the entire day, and then we picked up a puncture on the second last stage, we slid wide on the stage and burst the rim and dropped 50 seconds. That's rallying.

"Leg 3 was a big stage to start with, the first 5km had very slushy snow and our gravel crew had reported that it was really slippy. We were on winter tyres. We attacked the stage and it was a six right, it was a six right all day long, flat-out in our notes and we slotted down a gear and the car just took off and we went off the road, we hit the bank and it pushed us into the bridge at 100mph. We rolled twice/three times and the car was absolutely destroyed. Morale was dented and then to make matters worse we found that our rivals had suffered too, Hanninen went off on the first corner and Freddy Loix got a puncture, three out of the top four had problems. It was just unfortunate that it was reverse seeding and we went off on that corner. We have discussed it, it was experience as well, it was a fairly bad accident and even Kris got scared as he had no control over it.

"It was a big disappointment for everyone at home that we went out and that we would not get to the most famous stage in the world, the Col de Turini. Monte turned the tide and we dug in because there were a lot of critics at home, some were saying that Kris was back to his crashes again, and the general public were at it again. But we knew deep down that Monte was a mistake, it was out of our control and we knew we would have to dig deep.

"You get used to criticism, but yes it does hurt but you dig deep, we drive on and it makes you stronger. The Kronos team were obviously very disappointed as our car was destroyed. Peugeot UK was very disappointed but they saw the speed was there and the pace was there with the fastest stage time."

Chapter 10
Brazil – maiden win

Rally Internacional de Curitiba
05-07 March 2009
IRC Round: 2

With that crash from the Monte Carlo rally still fresh in the minds of Kris Meeke and Paul Nagle, the 13-hour flight from London to Brazil was never going to be the most enjoyable. However, it did give the boys and the rest of the team a lot of time to think on the criticism they'd received. There had been some, of course, but Kris and Paul were well aware of what had happened.

Meeke and Nagle head to Brazil for the next IRC event.
(Peugeot UK)

Kris – Brazil. (Peugeot UK)

Meeke contests Brazil. (Peugeot UK)

However, there wasn't just the criticism to contend with – the car had been badly damaged, and Kronos didn't have enough time to repair it before it had to be shipped to Brazil. This meant that Kris would have to drive the car with which Sebastien Ogier won the Monte Carlo rally. Kronos stated that there would a be a new car ready for the next round in Belgium.

Kronos Racing Team Principal Marc Van Dalen said: "It is no problem for Kris to drive the Ogier car because all the Kronos-prepared cars are the same specification, so it will be easy for him to change cars. It may even provide him with some good luck, because, not only is it the car Ogier used to win Monte Carlo, but it is also the same car Juho Hanninen used to win Rally Russia."

With more time to prepare for Brazil, Kris had a three-day test with Peugeot Sport in France. This allowed time in the car on gravel stages and working with Peugeot Sport engineers to understand further what the Peugeot 207 S2000 could do. This would prove to be valuable on the gravel in Brazil.

Meeke takes the lead in Brazil. (Peugeot UK)

Panoramic Brazil. (Peugeot UK)

Swapping the ice and snow of Monte Carlo for the humid heat of Brazil takes a bit of getting used to, so Peugeot decided to allow the boys to spend some time in Rio de Janeiro so that they could acclimatise before the rally got underway. The stages around Curitiba are fast gravel stages, with blind crests and jumps, and the temperatures were set to be in the mid thirties.

There were a number of changes made to the car which had been used on the asphalt of Monte Carlo. The suspension has been raised so the car could pass over the uneven surfaces, clear potential obstacles, and provide enough suspension travel to absorb high speed jumps and bumps. The suspension was also softer to enable the car to flow better over the rough roads. Tyres were also changed to special gravel tyres, which were tougher in order to resist punctures, and they had deeper grooves to expel loose objects, dirt, and to clear surface dust.

With the cars sliding more on the gravel surface than on Tarmac, the size of the brakes were also reduced, as the gravel didn't provide as much potential braking as a Tarmac surface

would. The biggest challenge, however, would be the Brazilian heat. Rally 'shakedown' kicked off in 32°C of heat, and both Kris and his co-driver Paul found the conditions challenging.

Kris said: "We had a couple of days in Rio to acclimatise (laughs), that's what they say, and then we came to the Curitiba, Rally HQ. You need to come out a few days early to let your body adjust. Your body has to learn how to sweat, and it has to learn to take on fluids, to replace them, and take on the correct fluids as well. For sure you have to think of that, there are some stages on this rally that are 30km, and you have to be at full concentration at all times, if you are getting hot and bothered on the stage, then for sure you will make a mistake or something.

"We have done events as hot as this in the past, in Turkey and in Greece, but this is a different sort of heat, it is a lot more humid with the rain forests. Since arriving we have had a thunderstorm and I have never seen rain like it, the clouds opened and you couldn't see to the end of the bonnet with the rain. It was that bad that the wipers were useless, the stages

The heat is on. (Peugeot UK)

were flooded within five minutes, that lasted for 30 minutes and the stages are still damp today from the rain yesterday. When the sun comes out and it comes up to 35/36 degrees centigrade, it makes it very humid, so for sure we will be sweating a lot, but we should have to look after ourselves and make sure we are taking on the right amount of fluids to allow ourselves the chance to perform well."

Kris went on: "The stages on the rally from the recce are absolutely fantastic, absolutely beautiful to drive. Nice fast flowing crests. From my experiences, I have recced on most of the rounds on the WRC and competed on the majority, this is similar to Finland, Mexico, New Zealand, really nice and flowing and great to drive. All the drivers should enjoy it, but of course, when it is so fast and flowing, you have to be careful as well. All the guys came out of the shakedown stage with a grin on their faces, so everyone is really enjoying it out there. It will be an interesting battle."

Paul Nagle agreed with his driver: "The Friday stages are very fast and flowing compared with Saturday, as these stages

Meeke on the way to first IRC win. (Peugeot UK)

are a lot more technical but they are still tighter and twistier. But the 28km stage on Saturday morning will probably be the big stage on the rally. It is a fantastic stage, it flows from start to finish. If you get into a good rhythm then you can get a fantastic time and get a good result."

The boys were looking forward to what Brazil might bring, but Kris had time to reflect on his Monte Carlo experience: "I have no regrets about Monte Carlo, yes I had an accident which turned into a sizeable shunt on the last day of the rally, but we were within touching distance of the lead. I was really happy with my approach on that event and we simply got caught out on a very tricky section that claimed a lot of cars. I would like to think I will approach this event in the same way. Yes we have to try and make sure we get points, but I'd like to think I would start every rally, that I am making sure I get to the finish. This type of terrain should suit me, I really enjoy this fast flowing nature of the stages and crests, and I have good trust in my pace notes and on this rally quite a lot of it is blind, you know, so it should suit me. I am going to pick my own pace

Meeke flying high. (Peugeot UK)

Making a splash in Brazil. (Peugeot UK)

Quick checks. (Peugeot UK)

which I am comfortable with and not take any risks, and then we will see where we are, but if we feel comfortable with the car then there is no reason that we cannot be fighting at the front."

Starting fifth on the road, Kris immediately laid down the gauntlet to the other drivers by posting the fastest time in the first special stage. This was a shot across the bows to all the critics after the pair's Monte shunt.

Not happy with one fastest time, on the second stage they went for it again, and for the second time in a row it was Meeke and Nagle who topped the timesheets.

Watching the Peugeot UK car in action, you would never have realised that Kris hadn't rallied in a competitive and modern car on the loose since Rally GB in 2006.

After stage one Kris said: "That was a little messy, I stalled a wee bit on the start and the first couple of corners were not so good, but I got into a good rhythm after that and, I don't know, I haven't seen the time yet, so I don't know how we have done. For 20km it was nice and flowing but it was quite difficult

Mechanics at work. (Peugeot UK)

Kris: "The roads are like this Marc, I promise." (Peugeot UK)

out there, it's like Finland [laughs] it can catch you out, you know you have these big blind crests into sixth gear corners and that extra 5mph that you could carry through, it will make the difference."

Paul said: "That was brilliant, very safe and steady, and he was very committed and fast on the stages, he is very committed on the notes, very, very enjoyable. That was a fantastic stage and we got off to the perfect start."

The big news from stage three was that Abarth driver Anton Alen had hit a rock and lost 41 seconds, demoting him to seventh overall. After stage 3 Kris admitted he had not competed on gravel for some time. He said: "The big thing for me is that my pace notes are working well. I have only done one rally on gravel in three years, and just to understand the pace notes and how to make them again takes a while. We're very happy; on the stage before it was uphill climbing and there was not much room to make up time. It is going very well, I do not know the time, but we were even faster going into this, and Anton Alen had a puncture, so that has maybe given us a cushion. I am delighted with the way it is going, this is a fantastic rally."

Stage four was more of the same for Meeke – four stages four stage wins – and this meant his lead in the overall standings

Cornering in Brazil. (Peugeot UK)

was now up to 27.8 seconds ahead of reigning IRC Champion Nicolas Vouilloz.

The pair were, as they say in rallying circles 'on it.' Five stages and another fastest stage time later, Kris, Paul and the Peugeot 207 S2000 were travelling at a fair rate of knots, and none of their rivals could touch them. Meeke's lead went up to 35 seconds.

Kickin' up dust. (Peugeot UK)

Jumping high. (Peugeot UK)

Kris and Paul took stages six and seven, and by the end of the seventh test and the close of day one, Meeke led the rally by 48.6 seconds; a dominant display. Kris and co-driver Nagle were in a class of their own.

So, at the end of day one, with Kris in the lead, how did they feel? The glint was back in Kris' eye. Smiling, he said: "Awesome, a near perfect day's rallying, absolutely fantastic stages, and the car has been brilliant. I have to say my co-driver has done a fantastic job, so, all-in-all the team is making my life very simple. All I have to do is push the pedals. But it has worked incredibly well. Now we have done the hard work, tomorrow we run first on the road and that is going to be very slippery so it will be very difficult tomorrow. Hopefully we have built up enough of a lead so we can hold onto that advantage tomorrow."

Starting first on the road was always going to be difficult as Kris swept the loose gravel off the stages for the following cars.

The first stage (SS8) saw Kris drop 11 seconds to the

Journalists surround Kris. (Peugeot UK)

Meeke flying in Brazil. (Peugeot UK)

fast charging Giandomenico Basso in the Abarth Fiat Grande Punto S2000. The choice of harder tyres against the softer tyres on the Fiat, and the disadvantage of being first on the road was clearly setting the rally up for a thrilling final day.

The next stage (SS9) saw Kris drop only 5 seconds to Basso, however, a further 11 seconds were lost on stage (SS10), so Kris's lead was reduced to 22.7 seconds. The crucial thing for Kris was not to lose too much time to Basso.

Meeke, was experiencing some problems: "The problem was that they put the refuel directly 100m after the stop control of a 30km stage and my brakes just boiled, so when we stopped the car, I had no brakes for the next stage." Kris got his brakes fixed after the mid-point service, and, after sweeping the stages clear, Kris was hoping for a fairer crack at the stages in the afternoon.

Kris was quite happy with his road sweeping ability: "Sweeping the road was not as bad as expected, it was very nice, we went onto a hard compound of tyre and I think some of the other guys were on the softer compound but it went very well. There was not as much loose gravel as I thought there would be, but it was still quite tricky in places. Running first on the road is not as easy, I definitely know what Freddy Loix was up against yesterday, but it's good. The only problem is

Paul, Kris and Marc. (Peugeot UK)

that the next two stages are going to be even more slippery, so we will have to be careful."

Kris fought back on stage SS11, when he took 12.6 seconds off Basso to increase his lead back up to 35 seconds. He also set the fastest stage time on SS11, taking his tally for the rally to eight fastest times. Kronos teammate Nicolas Vouilloz then moved into second place ahead of Basso by setting the second fastest time, as Basso spun on the stage.

Kris said: "I can't believe how clean the road is now, this morning we were the road sweeper but now we could feel such a difference. I think we have set a reasonable time, the lead is down to 23 seconds so we have to wait on Basso coming through, hopefully everything will go well."

SS12 saw Basso fight back, taking 4 seconds off Kris, but losing 3 seconds to Vouilloz.

Before the final stage, Kris looked in buoyant mood. "We are feeling very confident, for sure, I have confidence in the car, you just never know, the nerves can get at you and you begin to start hearing things, but we will try and keep it going until the finish."

Kris and Paul are triumphant. (Peugeot UK)

Nagle/Meeke winners. (Peugeot UK)

The final stage (SS13) saw Kris finish the rally in true style, setting joint fastest time with his teammate Nicolas Vouilloz. Basso dropped 16 seconds and finished the rally in third place after a fantastic fight with Kris and, later, Nicolas.

Kris' winning margin was 26.2 seconds over teammate Nicolas Vouilloz who, like Kris, bounced back from a disappointing Monte Carlo rally.

Giandomenico Basso was third, 47.9 seconds behind the rally winner.

It had been a very successful rally for Peugeot UK, Kris Meeke, and Paul Nagle, who, on their way to winning the Rally Internacional de Curitiba set nine fastest times out of thirteen stages, and secured Peugeot's second 2009 IRC win and the maiden victory for Peugeot UK.

An emotional but jubilant Kris Meeke laughed: "I feel incredibly sweaty after that, but now being serious, I have to thank so many people for getting me here, such as Colin McRae and his involvement in my career. The journey to Peugeot UK and the IRC has been a long one but I think this is a fantastic championship, many thanks goes to Peugeot UK for having the foresight to be involved and having me involved in it, also to all the other people involved back home that helped put this together, my sponsors who have stuck by me over the past few years, which got me out there and got my name in the picture, it has been a long time coming but it is just awesome to get the first victory in the IRC."

Co-driver Paul Nagle couldn't stop smiling, the Kerry lilt was in full flow and he admitted it had been a perfect rally and praised Kris' driving. "Brilliant for the championship, Kronos and Peugeot UK. Kris drove faultlessly and never put a foot wrong

On top of the world. (Peugeot UK)

from the first corner until the last stage. I think our accident in Monte made us stronger and made us work harder. No-one will ever know what happened on Monte except for me and him, it was a simple accident and they happen in rallying. We came here to prove a point and I think we did that. This was the perfect rally after Monte Carlo and we have proved a point, we have bounced back, and it was a perfect way to answer our critics."

Marc Van Dalen, Kronos team boss was delighted with the pace and the professional performance. "I am very proud, very happy, we have put in a lot of time and effort to get this Peugeot UK project off the ground and in a difficult time it is important to let people dream and have some pleasure. We are very proud for Peugeot and my team and the job Kris and Paul did, no mistakes, very clever driving, very happy."

This meant that after the first two rounds of the series Kris and Paul lay in joint second in the championship.

Celebrating on the podium. (Peugeot UK)

Spraying champagne. (Peugeot UK)

Rally Internacional de Curitiba results – IRC

1	Meeke/Nagle	Peugeot 207 S2000	2h08m05.7s
2	Vouilloz/Klinger	Peugeot 207 S2000	+26.2s
3	Basso/Dotta	Abarth Grande Punto S2000	+47.9s
4	Loix/Smeets	Peugeot 207 S2000	+2m32.1s
5	Cancio/Garcia	Mitsubishi Lancer Evo 9	+5m20.0s
6	Tulio/Valandro	Peugeot 206 S1600	+19m04.0s
7	Tedesco/Furtado	Fiat Palio1800	+20m53.0s
8	Tokarski/Gavieta	Peugeot 206 S1600	+21m48.8s
9	Valandro/Valandro	Volkswagen Golf	+32m24.7s
10	Fonseca/Cortes	Peugeot 206 S1600	+42m16.3s

Nagle's notes

"We went to Rio for a few days to acclimatise, and sure we enjoyed ourselves for a few days, sure you have to enjoy yourself when you're in Rio. It was a lovely relaxing time, and we did all the tourist things. It was good to get away from home and to get to Brazil.

Brazil flag and winners. (Peugeot UK)

"A brand new rally and we knew this was ours for the taking as no-one had recced it before, because all the other rounds, sure everyone knows them inside out. So we went to Brazil and the recce was good. Pressure, I wouldn't say there was pressure on us, but we knew we couldn't make a mistake.

"On the shakedown we took a bumper off and Marc Van Dalen was not too happy, we were taken into the naughty room and received a telling off. We made a couple of silly mistakes on the shakedown but we felt good about the rally.

"On day one of the rally we had seven fastest stage times, on a pace that no-one could match, and we got a good lead by the end of the first leg.

"But then we had to run first on the road the following day. The gravel was very loose on the first couple of stages and we learnt to control a lead of 30 seconds, we had more or less set the fastest times. On a couple we were beaten, but it was a rally we thoroughly enjoyed, it was a fast rally, a really ballsy rally, and it really suited us. It was brilliant to get over the

finish line on the last stage and get over the disappointment of Monte Carlo. To have 10 points on the board was a great feeling. There were a few tears from some of the Peugeot guys, they were very happy. To win so far away, the expectations were not make any silly mistakes as everyone had traveled so far. When we had come off one of the stages on the Saturday, we had a bit of Irish luck, I walked round the car and spotted that a tyre had come off the rim and we got it changed in time.

"Lady luck was smiling on us for a wee change.

"It is something I tend to do, just have a quick walk around the car and make sure everything is OK, especially on gravel rallies, I checked that and thought that's a bit of luck alright. Kris would normally check the tyre pressures but we vary the jobs, it was an enjoyable moment to be back on the podium and to be back winning again."

Peugeot UK did not send Kris and Paul to the Safari rally as the IRC works on a dropped score system, so the next event would be the Açores rally in early May.

Chapter 11
Two in a row

Sata Rally Açores
07-09 May 2009
IRC Round: 4

Where are the Açores? Kris: "I had to look at a map to see where I was coming to before I left the house to be honest with you, it is an interesting place."

The Açores is a group of tropical islands located in the Atlantic Ocean, the rally was to be held on San Miguel, and the changeable weather would mean that this event would prove to be a stern test.

Kris was in relaxed mood and spoke about his first win in the IRC and what the Açores had in store for him and Paul: "That achievement was probably the biggest win of my career, there's so much pressure on you when you are doing it. It was only really when you get home and you look back that you properly enjoy it, you know, we want that feeling again, that's the important thing.

"We have to work hard and keep working at it, we were obviously quite strong in Brazil, and we were quite confident with the car, but you know this rally is so different, it is a lot more technical, a lot narrower, you are traveling down some narrow lanes covered in thick gravel, and there are stone walls on each side of the road. Any little mistake at all could cost you dear. It is going to be very tricky, as I say, road position is going to play a big part in the rally."

Conditions would likely play a big part, as a mixture of weather was experienced on the recce and shakedown.

Paul Nagle's first look at the stages reminded him of some he had rallied in the UK and Ireland: "It is all a bit narrow, very like home, it's a bit like Scotland and Ireland. They are very, very tricky, there is no room for error, as the stages are so narrow, but we are looking forward to it. It should suit us, it should suit us more than Brazil. We'll see. It is going to be difficult as one side of the island yesterday was nice and sunny but when we went to the other side of the island in the afternoon it was pouring with rain. It is going to be hit and miss with tyre choice, as it's a tropical island and the weather changes so quickly from one end of the day to the other. That could be a big problem, running first on the road could be a big disadvantage for the Skodas, so our road position looks pretty good for the rally."

Could Kris and Paul win again?

Marc Van Dalen: "The big problems will be the Skodas. The local drivers are very strong, but I am quite confident as Kris is trying enough now to be on the pace. But we have to think about the championship, and we want Kris to finish in the top three to be in a good position for the championship. We will see after the first few stages where we are and go from there."

The SATA Rallye Açores for Kris, Paul and Peugeot UK began the way Brazil had finished, the guys were in confident mood and showed they would be going for another win.

The first stage of the rally was a 1.7km super special and it was a 1, 2, 3 for Peugeot, with Loix leading from Meeke and then Vouilloz.

When the Peugeot UK team got onto the 'real' stages, Kris Meeke continued where he left off in Brazil, roaring into the lead on the second special stage. Kris referred to his pace as 'driving comfortably.'

SS3 Sete Cidades saw Kris set the first fastest time, and increase his lead over Juho Hänninen to 2.8s. Juho,

A happy Kris in Açores. (Peugeot UK)

Shakedown Açores. (Peugeot UK)

Shakedown Açores 2. (Peugeot UK)

Paul and Kris chat on shakedown. (Peugeot UK)

SS1 Açores. (Peugeot UK)

Up and at 'em in Açores SS1. (Peugeot UK)

Freddy v Kris. (Peugeot UK)

unfortunately, managed to hit a wall at the end of the stage, damaging the right-hand rear side of his Skoda. The impact was sufficient to drop him down to 38th position by the end of the next stage, SS4.

Paul Nagle brought us up to date on the morning loop before an errant wheel became the talking point, Paul explained: "SS2 was difficult, we stalled on one junction, it was a very slippy stage, a lot worse than we thought, at one point it was so slippy, that we couldn't get stopped, the car locked up and we dropped two or three seconds with an overshoot. We still set a reasonably good time, and we were afraid that we had a puncture on the stage as well. The dust was hanging in the air for us, and we maybe dropped a couple of seconds with that as well. All in all, a reasonably good stage. SS3 was a fantastic stage for us, we drove exceptionally well, then we heard Juha went off right on the flying finish and hit the back of his car."

By SS4 Meeke had eked out a lead of 13 seconds over fellow Peugeot driver Nicolas Vouilloz, as the Dungannon ace

set another fastest time. But it could have been a different story. Towards the end of the stage Kris hit a rock which wasn't in his pace notes, and damaged the right-hand rear wheel. Unaware of the damage Kris pressed on, only for the wheel to fail completely as the car slowed for the stage end time control.

The drama continued as the damaged wheel came off, bouncing its way through the time control as Kris and Paul looked on, dumbstruck. The lads collected their jaws from the floor of the 207 S2000 and quickly changed the wheel, picked up the damaged one, and got going again.

The luck of the Irish was certainly playing to the boys' advantage as they rumbled into service and got the car checked over. When Kris and Paul got their breath back they realised that they had been quickest on the last stage, even though they had to finish it on three wheels.

A relieved Kris Meeke said: "The second last corner was a sixth gear flat-out corner, and there was something like a big stone in the grass, we didn't see it on the recce, luckily it only

Meeke makes a splash in Açores ... (Peugeot UK)

damaged the rim and not the suspension but you know when your luck's in, that happens. But okay, we just have to keep the head down, we have a little bit of a lead but it shows how simple it can happen. Careful from here now."

Despite the problem, Kris remained in the lead of the rally. The guys carried out a hasty wheel replacement at the side of the road and then headed to service.

On the next test, SS5, Kris immediately got back into the groove and was just beaten to the fastest stage time by Jan Kopecky, by 0.1 of a second. However, the Peugeot UK car was faster than the Belgian car, and this meant that the Meeke/Nagle combination went 1.3s faster than Nicolas Vouilloz. This, in turn, increased Meeke's lead to 14.5s.

Special stages six and seven were an all Peugeot affair, Freddy Loix was quickest on SS6 for the Belgian outfit, while Kris regained UK honour when he topped the timesheets on

... and demolishes the opposition. (Peugeot UK)

SS7. Meeke had now opened up a lead of 22.9s over Nicolas Vouilloz.

After service Kris and Paul headed back for their second run through Feteiras SS8 and another perfect performance saw Kris again set the fastest time, increasing his lead over his teammate to 27.1s.

The second run through Sete Cidades SS9 saw Kris set the fastest time of 10m 12.3s, increasing his lead to 31.1s, while

the final stage of the day, and the second run through Pinhal da Paz SS10, saw Meeke take it a bit easier and complete the test with the sixth fastest time. This still let Kris open up the lead to 40.2 seconds after the first full day of competition. SS10 was dramatic when it came to considering the IRC title, Juho Hänninen crashed out heavily in his Skoda, a big blow for the Czech outfit.

Meeke was 'on it,' though, and it looked like Açores was

Flying high in Açores. (Peugeot UK)

becoming a repeat of Brazil. Nobody could get close to Meeke and Nagle.

As the first day of the rally drew to a close, Kris was pretty happy with his day's work: "Yeah it has been a long wait for the last stage as, unfortunately, Hanninen had an accident, but yes it has been an excellent day. Have to wait and see what the times are like for this stage, but we think it is reasonably good, a good day at the office, it is the same as Brazil, we have built up a bit of a lead and it will take maximum concentration to try and keep it there for tomorrow."

Açores – Meeke. (Peugeot UK)

(Opposite) Açores – Meeke tries hard. (Peugeot UK)

61

A splashing good time. (Peugeot UK)

Kronos team boss, Marc Van Dalen was happy with the performance of Meeke and Nagle but was aware that the changeable weather could make the rally even trickier for the crews. "The weather could be tricky, if you are first on the road then it could be an advantage, today dry and tomorrow rain would be good for us, I am quite confident."

As dawn broke on day two of the SATA Rallye Açores, Meeke and Nagle were in contention for their second win of the season. The weather, as expected, turned and driving rain and strong winds welcomed the crews at the start line on stage 11, Ribeira Grande.

Thanks to the enthralling drive Meeke put in on day one, this meant the UK car would start as first car on the road. SS11 was another one for the record books, Meeke set fastest time as he widened his lead over his rivals.

Cornering. (Peugeot UK)

Stunning. (Peugeot UK)

Kris was relieved to get out of SS11 in one piece let alone setting the quickest time: "That was very tricky, there was a stretch of cobblestones in here, and it was just like being back in Monte Carlo, zero grip, so eh, I took it very steady, I think I got near enough the maximum grip, if anyone tries to take a chance then I think there is going to be a move, but okay, I am still here and I am happy."

Nobody could cope with the pace of Meeke, and the Dungannon ace widened the gap at the top of the timesheets by another 3.8 seconds, giving a total lead of 44 seconds after 11 stages over Nicolas Vouilloz.

SS12 was the longest stage of the rally so far, the 21.78km Graminhais stage. The time sheet, however, was getting repetitive – yes, Meeke and Nagle were fastest again. There was a change in second place, though, as Vouilloz dropped

Meeke leaves rivals in his dust. (Peugeot UK)

Meeke and Loix enjoy the banter. (Peugeot UK)

time, promoting Skoda driver Jan Kopecky into second overall. It was a bad stage for Giandomenico Basso, too, as he retired with suspension failure.

The next test, SS13, at 22.37km, was the longest stage of the rally. Meeke took it in his stride and set another stunning time. The Peugeot UK car was 'flying,' and Meeke was out on his own, but there was an intense battle between Kopecky and Vouilloz raging further behind.

The second run through this stage, Marques SS14, saw conditions change for the worse. Meeke was hampered by the weather and came home with the seventh fastest time, Jan Kopecky reduced the lead by 14.6s, to 51.3 seconds.

The weather was slightly better on SS15, and Meeke set the third quickest time on the test, but he did lose a further 4.1 seconds to Kopecky.

Jan Kopecky set the fastest time in his Skoda on SS16, with Kris setting the seventh fastest time. The lead was now 44.5 seconds with two stages left.

Mechanics get to work on the 207. (Peugeot UK)

The competitors were told midway through SS17 that it would be the final stage of the rally, as SS18 had been cancelled due to standing water in the stage. To make sure of the win, Kris got back 'on it' and set another fastest time and took the rally win by 53.1s from Jan Kopecky.

A jubilant Kris Meeke said: "Yep, this is fantastic, it has been a very difficult weekend, it was a very tricky rally, but okay, we were able to set the pace just like Brazil. In these treacherous conditions it wasn't easy to control, but I have to say I rank this one above Brazil. Every one was here, the Skodas and the Abarths, everyone, so it is fantastic to get the win. This sets us in right shape going onto the Tarmac events, so we'll see. This has put us right back in the hunt for the championship title, with two maximums now, with the dropped score system coming

Nicolas Vouilloz and Kris. (Peugeot UK)

Between the stages on public roads in Açores. (Peugeot UK)

The Rallye Açores podium. (Peugeot UK)

into count then we're sitting pretty good at the moment, but hey, there is a long way to go."

A happy Paul Nagle was delighted with the win: "This was a better win than in Brazil. A near perfect rally, it is sweeter than Brazil with all the competition here, with Skoda, Abarth, and the local boys here. This is a great result for us. Kris drove inch perfect from the first stage to the very last corner. We led the rally from start to finish just like Brazil, and he was in a class of his own this weekend."

Where there any nerves on the final day?

Paul said: "Aaaah, there were a few nerves this morning, the weather was not too good, lots of fog and lots of rain. But we drove steady, middle of the road, no problems, couple of bumpers that's all. Just a bit sweeter than Brazil, two in a row is good."

Marc Van Dalen knew Meeke would deliver for the team after a dream start to the championship: "I know how quick Kris is. I mean, I was quite confident for the season with Kris as I

have known him for a while. I also know how strong the 207 is. All the cars are very strong also, as are all our drivers, Kris and Paul both did a great job this weekend. The weather conditions were very difficult. Okay, second victory in a row and leading the championship is very important for the future."

Kris now lead the championship by two points from Freddy Loix.

Final results (after SS17):

1	Meeke	2h36m48.3s
2	Kopecky	+53.1s
3	Vouilloz	+1m04.8s
4	Loix	+2m15.2s
5	Peres	+4m45.2s
6	Wittmann	+5m33.2s
7	Rautenbach	+5m35.8s
8	Moura	+5m41.3s

Kris and Paul on the winning step in Açores. (Peugeot UK)

Nagle's notes

"Another new rally for us, we knew our car was quick, but then we had Skoda coming as well, so it was going to be a really competitive rally. We knew Hanninen was quick on gravel, he was the man to watch in the Skoda camp, we had an idea Jan Kopecky wouldn't be as sharp, he is a very quick driver but Hanninen would be the man to keep an eye on. We just didn't know how quick the Skoda would be on gravel. We had heard the reports and the news from testing, but we just didn't know. The recce was grand, but anyone who watched the coverage on Eurosport, well you could see the drops were horrific. Luckily for us we couldn't see the drops, as the banks were so high, Kris told me how bad the drops where when we were flying home. I thanked him for that (laughing).

"The first day was good, but on the super special we had a sloppy time, a combination of complacency and things just not clicking for the both of us. It was just a bit sloppy. We just didn't get into the way of things as quickly as we would have

liked, and it may have been a hangover from the success of Brazil. Super specials are frustrating, you'll never win a rally on them but you can lose a rally on them.

"But on the first proper stage we were joint fastest again, and then on the next stage Juho went off, he took the wheel off across the flying finish. We were fastest on the rest of the stages on the Friday, and we were really happy with that.

"Then on the Saturday morning there was rain, fog, and everything. It was like home and running first on the road was a big disadvantage out there, as the rain went into torrents on the roads and it was like floods.

"We took a bumper or two off through these, and we were disappointed about that, and taking them off meant a couple of visits to the naughty room when we got back to service.

"We were dropping a lot of time on one stage. But there was one big stage where it was twenty something km long and we were fastest by a second a km. We didn't make an effort, it was like simple driving, pure relaxed, turn into junctions,

Meeke winner of Açores. (Peugeot UK)

A trophy-laden Meeke. (Peugeot UK)

don't go on the power too early, we ended up fastest but it felt so slow.

"The second last stage of the rally was all fog, and you couldn't see the end of the bonnet, that was a bit nervy through there for the first seven or 8km, and then the fog cleared and the stage got better.

"Kris doesn't like the fog, but he did well and he has very specialized notes. Our notes are very complicated 1 to 6 with 6 fastest and every corner is over a distance, minus for braking and plus for accelerating and as the year progressed, we started using open plus and push and OK and STOP. Sometimes you could have two lines of notes for one corner.

"This can be difficult to get all the notes out in time, I only stay one corner ahead of Kris, rarely it would be two corners. I have to mind him sometimes as he can get carried away at times.

"The last stage in Açores, we got splits in the car so I knew we were okay, and we got through the stage and it was a fantastic feeling to win two on the trot, two gravel rallies, we were very, very happy."

Chapter 12

Three in a row – Meeke hits his stride

Belgium Ypres Rally
18-20 June 2009
IRC Round: 5

Ypres is a classic in rallying terms, and it's just about impossible to win the event on your first go. So what would be the objectives for Kris and Paul on their first visit to the classic stages?

The drama began on shakedown, Kris and Paul would be going into the naughty room, as they arrived back with only three wheels on the car. There seems to be an ongoing theme: Kris and Paul find the limit on shakedown and then win the rally; well, it happened in Brazil and on the Açores. Could they honestly win in Ypres?

Kris, the IRC Championship leader, said: "These Belgium roads are quite specific, if you slide wide even six inches then you are going to touch something, and then you are out of the rally. So, I think it is a lesson learnt with our run on shakedown, we have a lot to learn on this rally, and with our championship position and Freddy's experience on this event, we may have to accept third or fourth place. A good haul of points would be nice rather than gunning for victory, to beat these guys on their home patch is next to impossible."

Kris added: "I want to win the championship and you don't necessarily have to win all the rallies to do so, and I think this one is one of the most unique of the season. The roads on the recce look quite simple to the naked eye but where the guys are taking the cuts and where they are carrying the speed is amazing. It is so specific and you need lots of experience in knowing when and where to cut. But we have to learn and we have had three passes on the recce, but when you take it that

Marc Van Dalen chats to Paul Nagle. (Peugeot UK)

69

Meeke tackles Ypres. (Peugeot UK)

Freddy has done it 14 times prior to this, we will be up against it. I am looking forward to the challenge."

The Peugeot pair would get their first IRC stages in the dark on Ypres, and the likeable Nagle was up for the challenge: "Two stages in the dark, will be very difficult for us, as they are used every year for the last 15 years. There could be a problem with knowledge in the dark, as obviously we won't see as much as you would in daylight. But we are looking forward to it and we usually go pretty well in the dark. The cuts on where and when you can cut are a big advantage to the locals here. We have changed our notes four or five times according to the different cuts, hopefully we have them all in, and hopefully they are all right."

Paul continued: "The weather has been fantastic all week, but on Friday there is a 40 per cent chance of rain, and

On song in Ypres. (Peugeot UK)

Roaring the green fields of Ypres. (Peugeot UK)

then on Saturday there is a 50 per cent chance of rain. But the locals are saying it is not going to rain, we will just have to wait and see, that should make tyre choice an interesting topic of discussion.

"In the IRC there are a lot of tyre options when compared to, say, a WRC round. We have a slick tyre on Tarmac, which at the moment looks like the tyre that we will start on. If it is kind of damp, we will go for a cut-slick, this is a slick with little cuts on the side of the tyre. It will be all up to what the weather does."

There was drama on the first stage, but it was one of Meeke's rivals that had been caught out. Francois Duval crashed out of the rally on the first corner of the event due to cold tyres, a shame for the home fans. Meeke kept his cool and set the quickest time on SS1, driving 1.4 seconds quicker than local hero Freddy Loix.

On the second test of the rally, Hollebeke, Freddy Loix beat Kris by 5.3 seconds, who, in turn, set the third fastest time on that stage.

Up in the air. (Peugeot UK)

Reflecting on seeing the Skoda of Duval parked on the first corner of the first stage, Kris said: "It was a bit of a shock to see Duval out on the first corner. We were very cautious, the time is probably not so good, but hey, I would rather be here than in Duval's position. Caution is the name of the game, the roads looks like they have grip, but it is so slippery out there, we went with a hard compound tyre, it gives you stability in some sections, but in other places the tyre is maybe not up to temperature, and the car is sliding a bit. However, I'm happy enough."

Despite Kris' 'cautious' approach, the Peugeot pair had set the fastest time, and had taken a surprise lead from local hero Freddy Loix. But Loix went fastest on SS2 and SS3. This gave Freddy the lead by 5.7 seconds over Kris after the evening's opening loop.

Cut cut cut – Ypres. (Peugeot UK)

The long and winding road ... (Peugeot UK)

Meeke negotiates a corner on Ypres. (Peugeot UK)

It was getting dark as the mid-point service came, and the light pods were fitted for the final loop of the day, the night-time stages. After a strong drive, Kris maintained second position overall throughout the evening, and was only 4.9 seconds behind Loix, with Jan Kopecky in the Skoda 8.4 seconds adrift in third.

Meeke was happy with how he and Paul had fared on the first day of Ypres: "The first day was exceptionally difficult, everyone talks about this rally and the cutting and the roads being so narrow, but for me the cutting was not so bad. The roads you can read, but it's the surface, I didn't appreciate how much the surface changes from km to km, and sometimes you go to brake and the car starts sliding. I cannot emphasise how difficult the roads are to read, as it all looks the same, some places are just so slippery, there is like a very, very fine sand on the road, you cannot see it, but the second pass was a lot better for us.

"I don't think it is possible to beat Freddy here, in the dark maybe (he laughs), but not in the daylight. I think Freddy drives at the limit of the road, if you are able to match him, then it is as much as you can do, and to take time off Freddy is nearly impossible to do. So tomorrow I expect him to creep away again; one, two seconds. Tomorrow is like a completely new rally, as we don't know the roads, like I do this evening.

Meeke/Nagle drive well in Ypres. (Peugeot UK)

Meeke and Nagle prepare for a stage on Ypres. (Peugeot UK)

We have to learn tomorrow where the slippery sections are on the first pass, and then see what happens."

Marc Van Dalen was pleased as punch with the prospect of a 1-2 on his hands: "I know that from the beginning of the year that Kris is very fast everywhere, so it is not a surprise to see him fighting for the lead. Ypres is a very special rally, but he deserves a lot of credit for his drive so far, if Kris and Freddy don't make any mistakes then we can be in the top two positions at the end of the event."

With the chances of rain increasing, Marc Van Dalen was not at all worried: "We like the rain, we have a lot of experience with the tyres. We are from Belgium, if the conditions change we will be able to react."

The second day of the rally kicked off in dry conditions with Kris ninth on the road. He was immediately followed by overnight rally leader Freddy Loix. Day two stages were completely new stages to the drivers, so there was no experience for Kris to fall back on.

However, Kris' big rival and Peugeot teammate Freddy Loix was completely at home in the stages, as he'd driven them many times before.

But fans of Kris should not have worried. New stages and Kris setting fastest times has been quite common in the IRC in 2009, and the seventh stage on Rally Ypres was to be no different. Yes, Meeke had done it again, he left the Langemark test as the quickest car and the lead was now reduced to a gap of two seconds from the 4.9 it had been before that test.

Kris explained that SS7 was very tricky: "Incredibly slippery on the opening stage, it was so, so fast on that first one, it gives you less time to read the grip, it was interesting, but I'm trying to shut the race out of my mind and drive my own rally. The guys are all going at a very good speed, and we are trying our best but I am not thinking about position, even if we go slowly on one stage and we get third position it will still be good. I'm trying to shut the race out of my mind and drive my own rally."

Meeke makes his way through the lanes of Ypres. (Peugeot UK)

Cutting corners in Ypres. (Peugeot UK)

On stage eight, the rally lead was getting intense, Freddy and Kris were swapping times at the head of the table, this time it was Freddy's turn to go quickest, the gap was now up to 3.5 seconds. Further down the field, Skoda's Juho Hanninen had powered his way past Abarth's Giandomenico Basso into fourth.

SS9 was another stage win for the likeable Belgian Loix, but this time he was only 0.2 seconds quicker than Meeke. This did mean, though, that the lead had increased to 3.7 seconds.

There was drama for Meeke's rivals, reigning IRC Champion Vouilloz left the road on SS9 and was out of the rally. Vouilloz was trying to get past Michael Solowow's Peugeot, which was slow thanks to a puncture, Vouilloz was being held up and he was losing time. He was too eager trying to get by Solowow and went off the road.

Meanwhile, the Skoda of Jan Kopecky, when travelling between SS9 and service, was hit by a motorcyclist. All involved were unhurt, Kopecky didn't lose any time, and he made his way back to service in third overall.

Back to the action on SS10, and the battle for the lead was engrossing, Meeke went quickest and brought the gap down to 1.6 seconds.

Stage 11 saw Meeke and Nagle at the top of the timesheets, and this time they had brought the lead between themselves and Freddy Loix down to 0.2 of a second. Meeke was proving to be a formidable opponent in Freddy's back yard – to be competing at this pace on your Ypres debut was a stunning piece of driving. Jan Kopecky put in a really good time and proved that he would be there or thereabouts, too, when the final positions were being sorted.

Meeke looking determined in Ypres. (Peugeot UK)

Paul looks quite relaxed at service. (Peugeot UK)

Kris enjoys the craic with BF Goodrich Drivers Team's Thierry Neuville. (Peugeot UK)

Kris explained that he didn't want to get into a fight with Freddy for the rally win: "I don't want to get into a battle with Freddy, but there's 0.2 after 200km. I am starting the stages and not thinking about Freddy. I just want to drive at my own rhythm, to my own notes, and see what happens, it has been working okay until now, at least now we have seen all the stages, but for sure, everyone goes a little faster on the second pass. It's going to be a long evening but an interesting one; we'll see. I am not going to change anything, just drive at the same rhythm, we'll be happy with first, second or third. If first comes, I'm happy; if it doesn't, I'm happy."

Paul Nagle commended Kris on his driving: "It's absolutely brilliant, but it's not half as good as it is in the car. The stages have been very good to us today, been in the middle of the road, keeping out of harm's way, and Kris is driving exceptionally well. 0.2 of a second, you can't even think of how tight it is, it is going to be a very interesting afternoon and into the night, as the final stage is at 21.30 hours. We drove very neat and

Servicing the 207 in Ypres. (Peugeot UK)

tidy, there were a lot of junctions, the idea on this rally is to be neat on the junctions. Between us, Freddy and Kopecky, there was 2.3 seconds over 30km. It's going to be an interesting last stage, it will go down to the wire definitely. A last stage dash, who knows?"

On stage 12 the lead changed hands as Meeke edged in front. Kris put in another storming time and led the rally by 0.8 of a second from the five-time Ypres winner.

The thirteenth stage changed the face of the rally and the pressure on Meeke eased a little. The drama was that Loix had picked up a puncture, dropping the Belgian to fourth, and promoting the Skoda pair of Kopecky and Hanninen into second and third respectively.

Meeke remained in command of the rally, but it was Loix who set the fastest time on SS14. Loix went quickest on SS15 as he set about trying to claim back a podium position. All Meeke had to do was hold the 24 plus seconds that he had from Kopecky, and the Dungannon ace would make it three rally wins in a row.

At the end of SS16 Meeke and Nagle were both emotional and jubilant, they had come, seen, and conquered in Ypres. It was simply amazing for the guys to win as Ypres rookies.

On the final 31-kilometre stage, Skoda's Juho Hanninen lost third place to Freddy Loix following a puncture.

So it was three wins in a row for Meeke and Nagle. An over-the-moon Kris bubbled: "Ypres is a very specialized event. I have only seen some videos and heard some people talking about it. You never really appreciate it until you come here yourself, even on the recce you think your notes are right, but you never know until you compete on the stages. I have to thank everybody in the team: Peugeot UK, Kronos, Peugeot Sport, and all the guys who have supported me, and this man here (pointing to Paul Nagle), he has been top."

Paul Nagle was a happy man: "We were getting the momentum going, it was getting close, and we were 0.8 ahead of Freddy before he went off and picked up a puncture. It was a fantastic battle, and credit to Freddy as well, he drove brilliantly, and to be 0.2 of a second after 250km that was phenomenal.

Kris chats to Freddy. (Peugeot UK)

*Meeke and Nagle roll into service as winners of Ypres.
(Peugeot UK)*

Rally Ypres winners. (Peugeot UK)

But to win this rally was just fantastic. Kris drove brilliantly, and the whole team worked like a well-oiled machine."

The final day of Ypres was on Father's Day, and Peugeot UK had brought Kris' dad over to see his son finish the rally. Kris said: "My dad never usually comes to the rallies as he thinks that we won't finish when he comes. I'm chuffed to have him here, it is great to celebrate with my brother Barry and my dad at the finish of what has been a fantastic rally."

Nagle and meek wearing their laurels in Ypres. (Peugeot UK)

Overall results after SS16

1	Meeke	2h32m16.3s
2	Kopecky	+20.4s
3	Loix	+1m40.5s
4	Tsjoen	+2m35.3s
5	Hanninen	+3m35.1s
6	Schammel	+4m06.4s
7	Van den Heuvel	+4m06.5s
8	Basso	+4m24.9s

Nagle and Meeke spray the champagne in Ypres. (Peugeot UK)

Kris now led the IRC Drivers' standings with 30 points over Freddy Loix on 24 points. Peugeot continued to dominate the Manufacturers' standings with 68 points, followed by Mitsubishi on 35 points, and Skoda on 25.

Nagle's notes

"There was a big time gap between Açores and Ypres, so we rallied in Barbados, and won the rally. it was nice to get away from the pressure of the IRC.

"The hype was starting to build from home and the UK, and Barbados was great to get away. At the start of the IRC season Peugeot had told us that a win and a podium would be great, but we had already surpassed those expectations. After coming home from Barbados, it was knuckle down for Ypres, and no one goes to Ypres on their first time and beats the Belgians on their home patch. It is such a technical rally, and so complicated, and we were told, 'you are not going to race' ... Kris was told, 'you have to do this and you have to do that.'

"Well, Kris went testing before the rally and was nearly two seconds off Freddy Loix and he wasn't happy. I wasn't there, Kris was on his own, but then we ended up a second quicker than him on shakedown. Kris kept saying, 'the pace is quick out here, the pace is quick, and I do not know how we are going to fare out here. On the shakedown we always seem to make silly errors.'"

Paul nervously chuckled, "We took the back wheel off, and we were pulled aside and then into the naughty room by Marc. Never a good thing!

"It was our own fault. We made the notes in the rally car, and on the second run we were checking the notes, Kris was

Paul, Jon Goodman, Kris – Number 1 in Ypres. (Peugeot UK)

Paul, Marc, Kris: number 1 in Ypres. (Peugeot UK)

heating the brakes and we were chatting through the notes and we weren't listening, and then the corner tightened and the car took off. He pulled the handbrake, and we took the back right-hand wheel off, and the whole suspension off the car; got to service and the corner was hanging off the car.

"So here we go, off to the naughty room and we got a warning from Marc, 'Lads, 95 per cent, 95 per cent.'

"Then we went out onto the stage, we were joint fastest, everything was within tenths of each other. So we didn't know what to expect on the Saturday morning, the first stage we came out of, we were fastest. From there and for the rest of the day we were up and down on the six stages, Freddy was setting a blistering pace, and we were hanging onto him, while Jan was thereabouts. Nicolas went off the road, the pace was frenetic. It went down to a three horse race as the Abarths were struggling. So it came down to the dark, and for some reason Kris flies in the dark.

"The second pass over the stages we had a wee edge, our notes are so good he doesn't need lights, he doesn't need daylight to go fast. It was all working well inside the car.

"On the second pass through the stage, in the dark, we pushed on a little harder as we knew our notes were perfect and we went quicker than we had been in the daylight.

"This put Freddy on the back foot, there was only four seconds in it, but the rivalry was intense, the atmosphere and the craic between ourselves and Freddy, it was just mega.

"We started the following morning, again fastest, and Freddy was trying very hard. There was a famous stage over Valence, 29km, we got to within point 2 of a second to Freddy after 250km. The splits didn't even matter, as there was less than a second here or there.

"Kris doesn't look at the splits, I tell him sometimes if I am comfortable with him, if not, I won't tell him. He does look down sometimes but rarely does he look at the splits. When it's that close I wouldn't tell him, but when we got the end of the stage I would say there is only point 2 between us.

"Freddy and Kris were laughing at each other and how close it was, but you could feel the tension in the Peugeot Belgium camp. It was a big rally for them, with Freddy being the local hero. He was enjoying it so much and he said to us that this was one of the most enjoyable days' rallying he has ever had. We went out the next day and went one second quicker than him and led the rally by point 8 of a second. We had heard from friends, who were spectating, that Freddy was getting very erratic, very wild, and then on the next stage he slid wide and got a puncture and had to stop and change it.

A contemplative Nagle in Ypres. (Peugeot UK)

Nagle takes a break on Ypres. (Peugeot UK)

"We were excited at the end of the stage, Jan Kopecky was still hanging in there, 17/18 seconds back, but to get into service leading Ypres with two stages to go was absolutely fantastic.

"We were the new boys coming to Belgium upsetting the whole thing, but Freddy took it in great spirits.

"With two stages to go, there was lots of tension around, you could feel that the mechanics and Peugeot Sport were all on a knife edge, we left service and headed to the stages.

"The last two stages were perfect, and I made sure from Marc that the last stage was definitely going to run in reverse for television purposes, so I knew Jan was in front of us and we could keep an eye on his times.

"So, we had to keep in touch with Jan, Kris drove middle of the road, no cuts anywhere, and I would tell Kris 10km to go, two seconds down, 6km to go, you're five down, you're okay, and we got to the finish and that was a fantastic moment.

"To win Ypres was unreal, it is one of the biggest Tarmac

A happy Nagle – Ypres. (Peugeot UK)

rallies in the world, you don't go to Belgium trying to win on your first time because you will have an accident.

"But it was brilliant, Kris' brother was there, as was Kris' dad, and to do it on Father's Day was just something else. That was the rally to win. There was a big party afterwards, which Freddy held with his fanclub. They all made Kris and myself feel really welcome, and they played *We Are The Champions*, Freddy brought us up onto the stage, it really was superb."

Having decided not to compete in Rally Russia, the sixth round of the IRC, Peugeot UK's Kris Meeke still lead the Drivers' Standings, but by just one point. Rally Russia was always one of the IRC rounds which Peugeot UK and Kris Meeke would not contest, so it meant a nail biting weekend watching the other S2000 competitors battle for the rally win.

Juho Hanninen finished the rally by setting his fourteenth fastest time and winning all the stages but one. Teammate Jan Kopecky came home in second.

Chapter 13
Experience counts

**Rali Vinho Madeira
30 July – 01 August
IRC Round 7**

It was nearly six weeks since the team's last round of the IRC in Belgium, but their performances in the shakedown and the super special stage, showed that Kris and Paul had lost none of their speed over the break.

So, what did Kris think of Madeira? He said: "It's a bit like every rally in the championship, it's new to me, and it's an interesting challenge. Madeira sounds like a very specialized and technical rally, when you get here and see the roads for yourself, it's like a Sanremo, but maybe even more technical. I would describe this rally as a clean simple rally.

"Tarmac roads with no surprises, every corner looks the same, it's just how fast to take each corner, and that comes with experience on these roads. It's probably the rally that resembles a race track the most. If you do laps and laps and laps, then you will be quicker. This is the first year they have really clamped down on the recce and only allowed two passes, whereas before, it all started out as an open recce, this will make it an exceptionally difficult rally. As I say, we just have to accept it and get on with it.

"A third place would be like a victory for me, six points you know, we put a lot of hard work in after Monte Carlo and managed to pick ourselves up again. Three victories in a row now, but I have to be clever, there's not much sense in trying to race the locals as they are Portuguese drivers, and Camacho lives on the island and knows it like the back of his hand. But he will not be in Scotland, Barum or Sanremo, so to go and race those guys would not be sensible. I have to keep an eye

Meeke prepares for the rally with his engineer. (Peugeot UK)

Meeke and Nagle race on the race track. (Peugeot UK)

on Freddy and Nicolas and Basso and see where they are at and manage the situation from there."

Paul Nagle was not impressed with the recce clampdown either: "We have had only two recce passes this year, whereas every year prior to this there has been four or five. This year there is an 80km per hour limit on the stage, and 50km per hour through the villages, so it has been pretty difficult for us as it is our first time here. You can get caught out very easily, it's not like Ypres where there are cuts, and changes in the surface. There is one surface here, and it is a glorified go-kart track, if you want. Along the side of a mountain, it's simple but it can catch you out, and you can lose time very quickly here. We expect a couple of the locals to be on top of their game, and they will probably take points, but we are happy enough to try and stay ahead of our main title contenders."

The Ralli Vinho Madeira was the seventh round of the IRC, and, as expected, the local drivers set the early pace on the shakedown.

Braking hard. (Peugeot UK)

Cornering at speed. (Peugeot UK)

The first stage was based around the port of Funchal, and it was only 2.18km long, but there were plenty of obstacles, including man-made 'chicanes.' It was a bit like a giant go-kart track, and the stage was very technical.

When the rally got going properly, however, it was championship leader Kris Meeke who was on top of the timesheets, 0.9 of a second ahead of current Portuguese Rally Champion Bruno Magalhães in his Peugeot. In fact, the French manufacturer was seemingly having a ball as its cars had eight positions in the top ten.

The first full day of rallying was never going to be easy for Meeke and Nagle, even though they had posted the quickest

Island backdrop. (Peugeot UK)

Madeira – flat out. (Peugeot UK)

Kris in deep discussion – Madeira. (Peugeot UK)

time on SS1. The pace was electric and it was Giandomenico Basso in his Abarth Grande Punto who led the way.

Meeke and Nagle seemed to struggle on SS2 and both of his Kronos teammates were quicker, it proved that experience of these stages would play a big part in the final outcome. This was apparent, as Meeke was again off the pace after SS3. In fact, he was 21.3 seconds slower than Basso.

Kris said: "I had a very bad SS2, I wasn't driving very well at all, I expected to lose more than 8 seconds. I had a better next stage, I was driving wiser. But all these corners are unbelievable, they are completely blind, you are in a narrow corridor, you have to trust the notes, if the notes are wrong then you are off the road, you know. It is very, very difficult."

After SS3 Basso had extended his lead to 4.1 seconds over Magalhães, with Camacho still in third. Kris was struggling and had dropped to seventh, 1.4 seconds behind teammate Freddy Loix who held sixth place, and 26.3 seconds behind Basso.

The second run through Campo de Golfe SS4 saw Basso again set the fastest time, 2.5 seconds quicker than his first run. Reigning IRC Champion Nicolas Vouilloz improved his time by

Pleased to meet you. (Peugeot UK)

87

Madeira – cornering. (Peugeot UK)

3.5 seconds to set second fastest time. Kris also improved his time when compared to his first run, but it was only by 0.7 of a second. This meant he set the sixth fastest time, beating Loix by 0.2 seconds. This was important as Freddy and Kris were having a real battle for sixth position. Kris remained in seventh, but was only 0.7 seconds behind Loix, and 30.9 seconds off the leader, Basso.

Stage five was a better outing for Meeke. He improved on his first run by 17.5 seconds, and was 8.1 seconds faster than Freddy. This meant that the Dungannon ace leapfrogged Loix and went up to sixth overall. Basso set another fastest time and was now stretching his lead at the top of the timesheets.

Basso's lead, as the cars returned again to service, had increased to 16.8 seconds over Magalhães, with Camacho a further 22.6 seconds behind. Kris, however, moved into sixth place ahead of Loix by 7.2 seconds, but still trailed Basso by 41.4 seconds.

SS6 Serra D'Agua saw Basso set the pace, beating Camacho by just 0.1 of a second and extending his overall lead to 17.1 seconds over Magalhães.

Meanwhile, Kris finished SS6 in sixth place overall, 43.8 seconds behind Basso. But he was quicker than title rival Loix, and extended the gap between the pair to 9.4 seconds.

SS7 Boaventura was another new test for Meeke, this saw him only get the seventh fastest stage time, Loix went quicker on this test and the gap between the pair was reduced to 5.6 seconds.

Basso was again quickest and the Italian extended his overall lead over Magalhães by 0.7 of a second, to 17.8 seconds.

Madeira – coastal roads. (Peugeot UK)

Madeira – an uphill challenge. (Peugeot UK)

Madeira, and a backdrop of houses. (Peugeot UK)

SS8 Cidade de Santana saw Magalhães set the fastest time, with Basso third fastest behind Camacho. This allowed Magalhães to reduce the gap to Basso to 16.9 seconds. Kris, again, was slower than Loix, so the gap between them closed to just 0.7 seconds. Basso was still rally leader.

Stage nine was another new stage for the UK team, and for Kris and Paul it almost spelt disaster. The 207 S2000 slid wide and then the crew damaged the driver's door – unusual, as rally drivers almost always damage the co-driver's side. The rest of the car was undamaged, but they dropped 4.2 seconds to Loix who moved back into sixth place, 3.5 seconds ahead of the UK car. Basso was again fastest, with Camacho second and Magalhães third. This meant that Basso had extended his lead to 19.1 seconds; he really was putting on a powerful performance.

The title challengers were at it again – Meeke and Loix were having a fantastic tussle. SS10 was the second run through Serra D'Agua, and Meeke went 4.8 seconds quicker than Freddy. This put the UK car back in sixth place. It really showed that when Kris went over the stages on the second pass, he was learning and getting much quicker. What would he be like with a few years' experience of Madeira?

Madeira – Meeke barges around the corners. (Peugeot UK)

Basso was again quickest on SS10, and the Italian increased his lead to 19.4 seconds.

SS11, the second run through Boaventura, was won by Magalhães, 2.1 seconds ahead of Basso, with Kris dropping down to seventh fastest. Loix was fourth fastest, closing the gap to Kris to 0.3 of a second. Basso's lead was cut to 17.3 seconds.

Under pressure from Loix, Kris pressed hard in the second run through SS12, Cidade de Santana, and set the fastest time in his Peugeot UK 207 S2000, the second stage win of the rally. Basso dropped to third fastest, and with Magalhães second fastest; his lead was reduced to 17.1 seconds. With Loix managing only fifth fastest time, Kris increased the gap to 2.6 seconds.

The final stage of the day was the second run through SS13 Referta, and this time Kris was third fastest, that second run was again giving him the experience and confidence he needed on this 'race circuit.' Kris increased his gap to Loix to 4.1 seconds, and reduced the gap to fifth place Rossetti to 4.1 seconds as well.

Madeira – getting points is enough. (Peugeot UK)

Madeiran crowds watch Meeke race around the island. (Peugeot UK)

The 207 roars into the distance – Madeira. (Peugeot UK)

Paul and Marc chat in Madeira. (Peugeot UK)

There was a surprise winner of SS13, Magalhães took the stage win, and with it reduced the gap to rally leader Basso to 16 seconds.

So, after twelve stages, Peugeot UK's Kris Meeke finished day two in Madeira in sixth place, 1m 7.7 seconds behind rally leader Basso.

Kris: "It just shows that, on the second run through, that we are matching the times of Basso and Magalhães; aye okay, that's Madeira, it's specialized and these guys are specialized in this type of surface. We have to take our time and learn, but it is nice to know that when we do get a chance, then we can be fastest. Very happy to nick a fastest time, but hey, all the time was lost this morning learning the stages so what can we do? We have to accept it. The worst thing to do is push and make a mistake, we have to think about the championship."

Marc Van Dalen: "Madeira is not a normal rally, it's more like truck racing, difficult corners that tighten, and I think Kris was surprised to see after the first loop how difficult it is. The only thing he has to do is to learn for the future, and to be at

Madeira sun – Meeke and Nagle. (Peugeot UK)

the end and catch a lot of points, because you need so much experience like Basso to be on top here. The most important thing is to stay on the road, and not make a mistake, if you make a mistake then you can damage the car really badly here. Kris has to push and stay on the road and needs to catch a lot of points."

Paul: "It has been a real difficult day, struggling on just two recce passes. On the first run this evening we have been swapping the top times with the other title hopefuls. The morale is down a bit, but the stage times this evening have cheered us up. We hope to get fifth as we are only four seconds behind Rossetti, and only four ahead of Freddy, so we have to push on. The stages tomorrow in the morning are new to us, so we will lose time there, but if we get fifth it will be a good result considering the whole situation this weekend."

Luca Rossetti in the Abarth Grande Punto claimed his first stage win of the rally, stage 14, while Giandomenico Basso, in another Abarth, maintained his overall lead.

The battle between Meeke and Loix was still raging. The Peugeot drivers were trading times at every stage. Freddy Loix went nearly two seconds faster than Kris Meeke, cutting the gap yet again.

Rossetti seemed to have had 'his Weetabix,' though, as he notched up another fastest stage time; that was two in a row. However, Basso was only 0.6 of a second slower, and kept a healthy gap of 15.5 seconds ahead of Magalhães.

Meeke on Madeira. (Peugeot UK)

93

Madeira – another stunning backdrop. (Peugeot UK)

Luca Rossetti had been flying, but it all came to a shuddering halt on SS16 when he crashed out of the rally. Basso remained in the lead of the rally, but the demise of Rossetti had promoted Meeke to fifth, while Loix was up to sixth.

This meant that Peugeot had eight models in the top ten.

On stage 17 Basso was back on top of the timesheets. He was in command of the rally as Magalhães was 17.4 seconds adrift of the Italian. Meeke remained fifth, while Loix was still within six seconds of the Dungannon ace in sixth.

There was drama on stage 18: Giandomenico Basso spun and dropped 10 seconds to second place Magalhães. With three stages to go, Basso would be very nervous after that hiccup. Meeke and Loix still remained in fifth and sixth respectively, with the gap staying about the same.

Stage 19 was a nervy affair, Magalhães was only 8.3 seconds adrift of the Italian, while the title contenders, Meeke and Loix were separated by just two seconds with two stages remaining.

Basso was coming under serious pressure, Magalhães took the stage win on SS20 and this reduced the gap to 7.6 seconds.

Kris Meeke's third-fastest time bought him a little breathing space from Freddy Loix, with only one stage remaining.

The final stage of the rally, SS21, saw Giandomenico Basso keep his nerve and win the 50th Rali Vinho Madeira by 3.5 seconds from Bruno Magalhães, the Portuguese driver closed the gap in the latter stages of the rally but just couldn't do enough.

Peugeot UK was more than pleased with the performance of Kris and Paul, as they demonstrated again, this time with an intelligent and measured drive on the very technical and specialist roads of Madeira, that they were real title challengers.

1 Basso	Abarth	3hrs 9m 55.4s
2 Magalhães	Peugeot	+3.5s
3 Camacho	Peugeot	+41.7s
4 Vouilloz	Peugeot	+49.4s
5 Meeke	Peugeot	+1m 21.9s
6 Loix	Peugeot	+1m 28.4s
7 Nunes	Peugeot	+4m 57.9s
8 Fontana	Peugeot	+5m 50.6s

Mountainous Madeira. (Peugeot UK)

Drivers' standings

1 Kris Meeke	Peugeot 207 S2000	34 pts
2 Jan Kopecky	Skoda Fabia S2000	29 pts
3 Giandomenico Basso	Abarth Grande Punto S2000	27 pts
Freddy Loix	Peugeot 207 S2000	27 pts
4 Nicolas Vouilloz	Peugeot 207 S2000	19 pts

Peugeot also extended its lead in the Manufacturers' standings.

Manufacturers' standings

1 Peugeot	82 pts
2 Skoda	43 pts
3 Mitsubishi (Ralliart)	41 pts
4 Abarth	34 pts
5 Proton	5 pts
6 Honda	1 pt

Madeira Super Special. (Peugeot UK)

Madeira – a marshal watches Meeke fly by. (Peugeot UK)

Meeke comes into service – Madeira. (Peugeot UK)

Nagle's notes

"After winning three in a row, the hype was really starting to build. Going to Madeira, the pair of us were confident, we had been to Belgium and beaten Freddy, and we would go here and take on Basso.

Kris and Paul finish in Madeira. (Peugeot UK)

"On the shakedown the times were good, they put a new engine in, a new medium gearbox was installed in the car, I wouldn't be up to date with the technology on the car, I was just listening.

"On Madeira we were only allowed two passes on the recce at 50km/h, whereas in other years competitors had been allowed quite a few more passes. The cut back on the recce was a big disadvantage, as Basso had been there the last eight years and he had won the rally on the last two occasions.

"All the locals knew it inside out as the national rallies use the same roads. We were happy with the two passes we had. Madeira is a fantastic island, probably one of the nicest islands I have ever been too, it's all corners, rock face, rock face, wide roads, narrow roads, it has it all.

"There are some third gear corners, some fourth gear corners, but when you're on a wide road, a third gear corner is a fourth gear corner. You use every inch of the road, and we struggled on that rally. I mind, after the end of the first stage, that Basso was eight quicker, and then on the second stage, he was another 20 seconds quicker, it was his experience of the island and his experience of the lines.

"Our notes changed a lot, and when we got through the stage, the toys were maybe flung out of the pram as we were lying seventh or eighth. Kris kept asking: 'What is going on here, we had won the last three, what is going on here?'

"The medium gearbox was too long for some corners and too short for others. We were struggling, and it was all about revs and carrying speed and we were just in front of Freddy and just right behind Nicola, it was the first time I think in two years, that Kronos weren't on the podium.

"For all of us it was a disappointing rally, but for me that was a championship-winning drive. We were beaten well. But I

On the Madeira podium. (Peugeot UK)

told Kris that was a championship winning drive, you wouldn't have done that before, we had a slide and blew a tyre, in a corner that tightened up. But to get through that rally with only a minor scrape was brilliant.

"Everyone was disappointed, but it was an accomplished performance. It kept us in the championship lead, and as I told Kris, we still have to go into the boys' backyards. We left Madeira leading the championship, but Basso was now a big title rival, and Freddy was still there, and Jan who didn't go to Madeira would be at the next round at the Czech rally. There was plenty to play for."

Paul Nagle agrees that a man's best friend is a dog.
(Peugeot UK)

Chapter 14
Points get you prizes

Barum Czech Rally Zlín
21-23 August
IRC Round: 8

The Barum Czech Rally based around Zlín (practically in Jan Kopecky's backyard) was a home rally for the Skoda team. For Kris and Paul, the aim of the game would be to try and score as many points as possible. This was going to be tough, though, as the Skoda cars would be hard to beat on their home turf.

With a five-point lead in the IRC Drivers' standings, Peugeot UK's Kris Meeke faced stiff competition from a total of 25 other S2000 drivers, including five Skoda Fabia S2000s, and eleven Peugeot 207 S2000s. A total of five manufacturers fielded S2000 cars in the rally: Skoda, Abarth, Peugeot, Opel and Proton.

Friday 21st August saw the ceremonial start of the rally, and then a three-lap, 9.36km Super Special stage in Zlín. The crews contested a further fourteen-all-asphalt stages over the next two days, with a total stage distance of 254.96km.

On shakedown, Kris and Paul had looked good, and were only a second adrift of Kopecky who, as expected, had set the quickest time.

However, drama was to unfold for the championship leader. Kris had not been feeling 100 per cent, and was forced to miss the pre-event press conference. The championship leader, along with the Peugeot team, decided it would be best for him to try and recuperate. This meant Meeke went off for an extended session in his hotel sauna, to try to sweat out the final vestiges

Super Special. (Peugeot UK)

Lots of air under the car in Barum. (Peugeot UK)

of his cold ahead of two days of intense competition. Meeke really needed to have full concentration as the Czech team was going to go all-out for a win.

The Czechs love rallying, and thousands of fans poured into Zlín (they had plenty of heroes to support, of course, as over 70 of the 107 starting crews came from the Czech Republic).

The first stage was a Super Special, and there was drama almost immediately for Meeke and Nagle, as the pair picked up a puncture as they clipped a railway track.

Kris was still feeling really poorly, so Paul Nagle set out their plan of attack, which was still to score as many points as possible in Zlín, and try to finish on Sunday ahead of their championship rivals, Kopecky, Giandomenico Basso, and teammate Freddy Loix.

Getting through the stages. (Peugeot UK)

Spectators in their droves watch Meeke.

Nagle stated: "Clearly the last thing we needed was the puncture ... now we've got it all to do to get into the points ... it's a tough order, but we'll be fighting."

With the opener over, the position of the Peugeot UK camp as to whether Kris and Paul would start in the morning was 'wait and see.' However, with the pair in 33rd place overall, 31.9 seconds behind the overnight leader, Finland's Juho Hänninen driving a Skoda, spirits in the Peugeot UK were gloomy as they headed for bed.

On the first full day of action, the doctor, as Paul Nagle so politely put it, gave a sneezing, shivering Kris "a stab in the arse" with an emergency flu jab, and it seemed to awaken the fighting spirit within him.

The 'stabbing' seemed to do the trick, and Meeke and Nagle started to haul their way back up the leaderboard. On SS2 the Peugeot UK car recorded the third fastest time, and shot up the leaderboard to 11th place overall. The comeback had started.

Sideways in Barum. (Peugeot UK)

Lifting a front wheel in Barum. (Peugeot UK)

Next up was SS3 Halenkovice. Kopecky took another fastest through the stage, 2.9 seconds quicker than Kris and 5.2 seconds quicker than Vouilloz. Kris jumped up to 9th; Meeke and Nagle were starting to fly.

Reigning champion Nicolas Vouilloz was to be the biggest retirement of the rally after his Peugeot 207 S2000 caught fire. The engine mounts broke, causing damage to the power steering system. With fluid leaking from the system, this then caught fire, and Vouilloz and his co-driver had to abandon the car. The Proton crew of Guy Wilks and Phil Pugh had been spectating at that actual spot, as they had suffered engine failure before SS2, and bravely helped to extinguish the blaze. Fortunately, the Peugeot crew were unhurt, but were unable to continue. Meanwhile, the flu jab was certainly working on Meeke as Kris set fastest time on the stage, and had now fought back to fourth overall.

Kris tackles the Barum stages on three wheels. (Peugeot UK)

Meeke contests Barum. (Peugeot UK)

SS5 was next, the second run through Pendulum, but it was not a happy hunting ground for Kris and Paul, as they spun, losing valuable time, and only managing tenth fastest.

Kopecky remained in the lead of the rally, and was 20.3 seconds ahead of Freddy Loix. Basso was a further 8.4 seconds behind, but Kris had dropped back to 52.6 seconds off the lead.

There was little change on SS6, the top four remained the same, but Kris did take a little time back.

As the cars came into service Paul Nagle was very animated. The big Irishman was sure that it was going to rain. Don't ask how he knew, he just did – an Irishman can smell rain. (Author comment 'We have it often enough, you can nearly smell it.') The Peugeot UK crew decided to take two full rain tyres as replacements in the boot.

Service in Barum. (Peugeot UK)

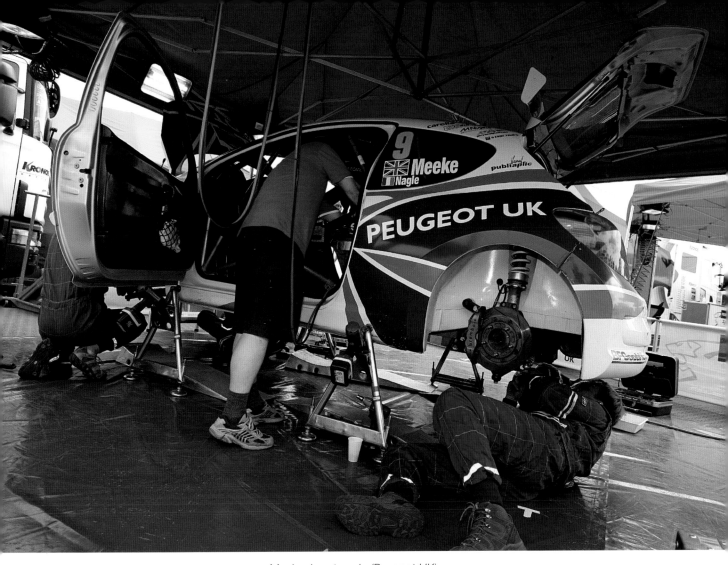

Mechanics at work. (Peugeot UK)

As the times came in from SS7, the first stage after service, some 'pundits' were asking whether the championship leaders made the correct tyre decision as Meeke had lost time, but the rain was getting heavier, and on SS8 they set joint fastest time with Jan Kopecky.

One of the big casualties in the rain was the Abarth Grande Punto S2000 of Giandomenico Basso, he had slithered off the road in the tricky conditions. Fortunately, both driver and co-driver were both OK, but their rally was over. Would this crash also end his title hopes? We would have to wait and see.

This promoted Kris Meeke and Paul Nagle up to third, and crucially, the man seen as their main rival for the title, Giandomenico Basso, was out of the rally and would not score points.

Working in the engine bay. (Peugeot UK)

At pace in Barum. (Peugeot UK)

The last run of the day was SS9 Avarice 2, and the rain continued to pour. Jan Kopecky took the honours on the stage to hold a lead of more than a minute going into the final day. However, just like at Ypres, it was shaping up to be a big final day fight between Kris and Freddy Loix. It may not be for the lead of the rally, but with just 8.4 seconds separating the Peugeot teammates, there was a second place to be won.

Meeke and Nagle had a brilliant day, starting in 33rd they had put themselves back in contention for a major haul of points as they headed into the final day in third position and closing in on Freddy Loix.

Realistically, Loix was the only driver Meeke and Nagle could overtake, as they were over a minute adrift of Kopecky. The Dungannon ace rocketed out of the box on the opening stage on the final day and set the fastest time on the test. Kris' road position meant he started behind Freddy, and, as they flew through the test, they spotted Loix's car by the side of the road. Damage following a puncture had put the popular Belgian out of the event. This meant that Kris and Paul were up to second overall, and eight championship points beckoned.

After SS10, Kopecky led the rally by 63.3 seconds from Kris, with Juho Hanninen a further 24.9 seconds behind. On SS11 Kopecky was fastest through the stage, 0.2 seconds quicker than teammate Hanninen, and 5.8 seconds quicker than Kris. This gave the Czech a lead of 69.1 seconds over Kris, with Hanninen closing the gap between second and third to 19.3 seconds.

SS12 at Komarov was a short 8.4-kilometre stage, and Meeke was certainly up for the challenge, Hanninen had been starting to turn the screw, but Kris responded in positive style

Lifting a wheel in Barum. (Peugeot UK)

So fast the crowd is a blur in Barum. (Peugeot UK)

by setting the fastest time. It was close, though, as the Finn came through just 0.8 of a second behind.

With only three stages remaining, the crews had a chance to recharge their batteries at the final service before putting in one last surge. Kris then set the fastest time on SS13, while Hanninen dropped time due to a spin, leaving Kris with a comfortable gap.

Stages 14 and 15 were pretty straightforward for the top three. Kopecky finished the rally with a hugely popular win, while Meeke and Nagle took second, with Hanninen in third.

Given the problems of the flu and the puncture at the start of the rally, to finish second in the overall classification was a brilliant result for the Peugeot UK team. This added another eight points to its championship haul, making it the favourite for the championship with three rounds remaining.

Cutting corners in Barum. (Peugeot UK)

Overall rally result

1 Jan Kopecky	Skoda Fabia	2hr 24m 21.1s
2 Kris Meeke	Peugeot 207 S2000	+ 1m 00.4s
3 Juho Hanninen	Skoda Fabia	+ 2m 00.8s
4 Roman Kresta	Peugeot 207 S2000	+ 2m 10.8s
5 Martin Prokop	Peugeot 207 S2000	+2m 39.6s

Drivers' standings

1 Kris Meeke	Peugeot 207 S2000	42 pts
2 Jan Kopecky	Skoda Fabia S2000	39 pts
3 Giandomenico Basso	Abarth Grande Punto S2000	27 pts
Freddy Loix	Peugeot 207 S2000	27 pts
4 Juho Hanninen	Skoda Fabia S2000	20 pts

Peugeot continued to lead in the Manufacturers' Standings:

Manufacturers' standings

1 Peugeot	95 pts
2 Skoda	59 pts
3 Mitsubishi (Ralliart)	42 pts
4 Abarth	34 pts
5 Proton	5 pts

Nagle's notes

"The narrow bumpy gravel lanes are like home (Irish Tarmac rallying features some of the best narrow, bumpy, and gravelly lanes in the world). The weather was iffy just like home, as you get anywhere in Ireland.

Kris showing Marc how he was lifting a wheel in Barum. (Peugeot UK)

On the way for a good points score. (Peugeot UK)

Professional drive. (Peugeot UK)

"Kris was complaining that he was sick all week, he was running a high fever and he missed the press conference because he was unwell. He was very sick and he clipped a railway track and we drove badly inside her (the car), and I said to him what's wrong?

"I knew he was sick but he didn't say much to me. There was sweat running off his face from the start line and he actually couldn't see from it, the sweat was running through him. We got through the stage and I changed the wheel, and he said nothing, and he got out of the car and he was sick and he said, 'Paul I can't continue, I'm not able.' He was frozen, then too warm, jacket off, jacket on, and then we got to service and put the car in the Parc Fermé, and we headed back to the hotel. He told Marc, 'I can't continue, I need to pull out in the morning.'

"Credit to Peugeot UK, Marc, and Christian, they all told Kris that if he didn't want to continue then he didn't have to, because health is more important. So Kris went off to bed and I went to my room, not knowing if we would compete in the morning.

Meeke interviewed by Eurosport. (Peugeot UK)

Muddy-looking. (Peugeot UK)

"I, honest to God did not think that we would start in the morning. I said to Kris, 'If you are not feeling okay in the morning don't worry we will not start.' But there was fight in him and he would have to be very sick not to start in the morning. So he got a 'stab in the arse' from the doctor, an eight inch needle in the bottom (Paul was laughing), 'a great big stab in the ass.'

"Kris kept getting better and the doctor kept giving him these bottles, the health was getting better, but we were still back in thirty third place, and all of a sudden we started punching in times and Kris was getting better. We started the second stage of the rally and came out with the second fastest stage on the first morning stage. I told the doctor, 'You keep giving Kris his medicine, it really is working. Give him plenty!' We kept climbing, climbing, climbing, and then Basso went off, a big pressure was lifted with that and we had fought our way up to fourth at that stage.

"The momentum was with us again, the morale was brilliant inside the car, and the rain was coming and we went out with

Delighted with Barum – Meeke. (Peugeot UK)

intermediates on and two full wets in the boot, while Freddy went out on slicks with intermediates in the boot, so one of us was going to have a mistake here.

"Freddy was 30 seconds ahead, and we weren't catching him, we were only taking a tenth here or a tenth there. But in the next two stages we were 'on it,' and we had made the right tyre choice. One of the stages was cancelled because Basso had an accident, so Freddy got a nominal time, which meant that Freddy was eight seconds quicker than us, we weren't happy about that. But sure that's rallying and it's the luck of the draw.

"We went through the next few stages and took 20 seconds off Jan and Freddy, and the gap to Freddy was down to eight seconds. We had a big spin on stage four or five, it was a spin in fifth gear, you don't usually get away with them, you know. It was a long four right on gravel, Kris got back on the power quickly and spun the car to face the right way and we got on with it, but we lost 15 seconds as a result. I just told him after

that to tidy it up (laughs Paul). By the end of the night we were 50 seconds in arrears, that was dropping 30 with a puncture and 20 with a spin, so we were happy with our pace. We knew Freddy was going to be fast, we had been scrapping with him everywhere all year. We decided to give it a go and I checked the splits on the first stage on the Saturday morning, Freddy after 12km was two seconds up on us, and I knew Kris was at 10/10 tenths, we were on a fair pace. Kris said to me, 'I can't go any quicker, I'll go off if we go any faster.' We hadn't gone 3km and Freddy was parked, he had clipped a rock and taken a wheel off the car, and he had knackered the suspension.

"We could smell rubber in the car and it was getting stronger, and then we passed Freddy's car, we didn't know what had happened, we thought he had picked up a puncture. Then we heard that Freddy was out of the rally when we got to the end of the stage. The next problem we had was that Juho Hanninen was coming flying behind us, and we knew we had to keep a good steady pace up. We just had to drive around,

Barum podium. (Peugeot UK)

stay out of trouble and keep Hanninen behind us. When we got to the end of the rally and finished in second place we were more than happy. Coming from 33rd up to second overall was a terrific result. To come back under that amount of pressure was probably the drive of the season, and there were only two non-Czechs in the top six – that's how quick the pace was at the top.

"The beauty of this championship is that anyone can score points. If you have a car and can compete against us then you can take points off us, which is great. I think this is a brilliant thing, if you want to win a championship then you should need to beat everybody. I think it should be kept this way."

Spraying champagne. (Peugeot UK)

Chapter 15
Nerves jangle in Spain

Rally Principe de Asturias
10-12 September
IRC Round 9

The next round of the IRC was the Rally Principe de Asturias based around Oviedo, the capital of the Region of Asturias in Northern Spain. The rally was round eight of the Intercontinental Rally Challenge (IRC), and saw Kris Meeke go head-to-head again with Skoda's Jan Kopecky.

With a three-point lead in the IRC Drivers' standings over Kopecky, the name of the game for Kris was to secure as many points as possible.

Oviedo is a mecca for motorsport fans in Spain, and also the birthplace of former F1 world champion, Fernando Alonso.

Stage one was fought in the dark, and Stage 2 was to be held as dawn came up. Fastest out of the blocks was local boy Alberto Hevia driving a Skoda Fabia S2000. Basso was 'on it' too, and was second quickest, Vouilloz was third, Kopecky fourth, while Kris and Paul were fifth fastest on the first test of the rally. Stage 2 was cancelled after Miguel Fuster went off the road.

On SS3, Kris and Paul were only 14 seconds off the lead, but then came near disaster when the lads picked up a puncture on SS4, costing them over 3 minutes, and dropping them back to a lowly 16th place overall. They now had a mammoth task in front of them just to pick up some valuable points.

Meanwhile, Peugeot teammate Nicolas Vouilloz won the stage, but Hevia retained his overall lead.

The stage at Cesa-Valdebarcena was to be run three times in the day, as SS5, SS6 and SS8. Hevia in his Peugeot

IRC calendar on the side of a truck. (SMcB)

111

Kris and Paul start in Spain. (Peugeot UK)

207 Super 2000 was again fastest, and after SS5 he led the rally by 2.6 seconds from Nicolas Vouilloz.

Kris and Paul got over the disappointment of the puncture on SS4 and got back 'on it.' Everything clicked on SS6 and they set the second quickest time on the stage; that was more like it. Meeke was now up to ninth and closing in on eighth placed Michal Solowow. Hevia continued to lead from Vouilloz, Basso and Kopecky.

With Basso and Kopecky in third and fourth, the pressure was on Meeke and Nagle to get as high in the placings as possible before the end of the day.

The boys notched up another second fastest time and with that, they took eighth place from Michal Solowow, again only Basso was quicker, and on this stage he took the overall lead from Hevia. There were more problems for the Peugeot camp as Freddy Loix suffered a puncture, losing over 2 minutes and droping from fifth to seventh.

SS8 was cancelled because of spectator overcrowding. On SS9, Skoda's Jan Kopecky won the stage and moved to

Kicking gravel as they go – Spain. (Peugeot UK)

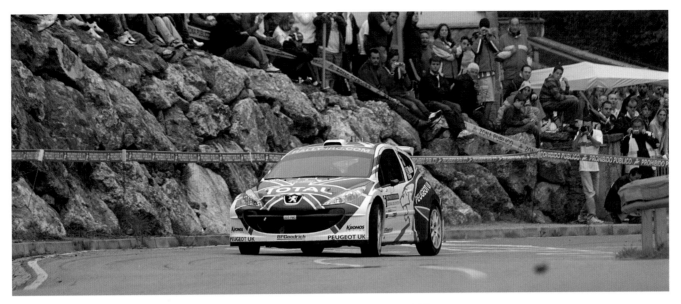

Meeke flies in Spain. (Peugeot UK)

207 up close in Spain. (Peugeot UK)

Meeke roars into the Spanish countryside. (Peugeot UK)

third, breathing down the neck of the Asturian rally hero Alberto Hevia. Meeke was coming, too, though, he secured another second fastest time and, by the end of the first full day's rallying, the Dungannon ace was up to seventh.

Paul Nagle was relieved to have made it back into the points after a bad start: "It has been a difficult day for us as we got a puncture on SS4 and we dropped three minutes. Tonight, we are three minutes off the lead, unbelievable. We braked 10 feet too late, slid wide, and then realised we had a puncture, and then stopped and had to change it. We have climbed from 14th to seventh, but Jan Kopecky is second and flying so it is not looking good at the moment. If Kopecky wins here then we are in big, big bother when looking at the championship. We'll just have to wait and see."

Kris was philosophical on that puncture and how the rest of the day had gone: "If we hadn't have had the puncture we may have been within ten seconds of the lead, but sure a puncture is a puncture, what do you do? Sure that's rallying.

Meeke/Nagle on course in Spain. (Peugeot UK)

Kris tackles Spain. (Peugeot UK)

Kris has a chat with Nicolas – Spain. (Peugeot UK)

Meeke in Spain. (Peugeot UK)

Tomorrow we will see where we are, just keep driving and try and take time from the boys ahead of us. I made a mistake, I got a puncture, I have to accept it and get on with it. We slithered under braking, and we had it in our notes as the road was greasy, and we just left the braking slightly too far and we slid sideways, touched the bank, and we got a puncture at the rear. We also had a problem with the injector on the engine, we had to change everything at service and that slowed us a little, but we got it all fixed at service. The asphalt is very slippy and very inconsistent, different every corner, but since lunchtime we have had three second fastest times, and we have probably been the fastest driver since stage 3 or 4, so it has been very good since then. Tomorrow I will push on and then we can go from there."

The final day of the rally began with Stage 10. Kris was on full attack and set the fastest time, closing the gap on Freddy Loix to just 7.4 seconds. Up front there was worrying news for the Peugeot UK team; Jan Kopecky went quicker than fellow Skoda driver Alberto Hevia, and leapfrogged the

Peugot convoy. (SMcB)

local boy and went up to second place overall. This meant that overnight leader Giandomenico Basso had a 12.1 second lead over Kopecky.

Basso kept the Kopecky charge at bay on SS11 as he increased his lead to 12.4 seconds, while Meeke, too, was also on a charge. He overhauled Loix to move into sixth place on the overall leaderboard.

SS11 at La Nueva was almost twice the distance of SS10. Basso kept the charging Kopecky at bay, marginally increasing his lead to 12.4 seconds. Kris did enough to overhaul Loix, moving to sixth overall, with Nicolas Vouilloz winning the stage.

There was high drama on SS12, the pressure got too much for Abarth driver Giandomenico Basso, the Italian spun off the road and into a ditch, and he lost seven minutes before he could get his car back on the 'black stuff.'

Basso. (SMcB)

Kris 'on it.' (SMcB)

Kris kicks up dust on Tarmac roads. (SMcB)

Kris laughing in Spain. (Peugeot UK)

This was good and bad news for Kris, as his main title rival, Jan Kopecky, was now leading the rally, with Kris now promoted to fourth place. Skoda driver Alberto Hevia lay second, 9.5 seconds behind Kopecky, while Nicolas Vouilloz was in third.

When Kris arrived into service he told of the fog that had been a problem up in the hills: "I was a little slow in the fog." A Spanish journalist asked Kris: "But you are Irish, you are used to fog?" Kris laughed and replied: "Even if you are Irish you cannot see in the fog. The first stage was misty, and then for 3km it was really thick fog on the second test this morning."

Paul praised Kris' driving: "We were fastest this morning on the first test out, and we put in a string of strong top three times after that. We are very happy and the Peugeot spirit is very good. Nicolas knows his championship is over, so he may give us a helping hand up the leaderboard; he does not want to jeopardise anyone in the Peugeot camp. Kronos and

Peugeot Belgium have said no to team orders, so it will be up to the drivers. We'll see what happens, as there are a lot of stages to go yet."

There was more drama on SS14. This time it was the local boy who would be hindered by a puncture. Hevia dropped to sixth place, which meant that everyone below him moved up one place. Nicolas Vouilloz and Kris would, therefore, finish on the podium, provided they negotiated the final stage. Kris was sure a black cat ran across the road ahead of him on stage 14, and certainly his luck had changed after the unfortunate puncture on day one.

SS15, the final stage of the rally saw everyone taking great care: the top eight finished as they started. A well deserved victory for Jan Kopecky, with Nicolas Vouilloz second, and Kris and Paul in third. However, back in the Service Park, Nicolas Vouilloz elected to check out later, taking a time penalty, and allowing Kris to move up to second overall and retain his lead

Another junction. (SMcB)

in the Drivers' Championship, a gesture that was warmly received.

There was more good news for Peugeot as the maker had now scored enough points to retain the IRC Manufacturers' Championship. This was the third year in a row that the title had been won by Peugeot, despite ever-increasing competition from other marques.

Into the dust. (SMcB)

Loix. (SMcB)

Overall results Rally Principe de Asturias

1	Skoda Fabia S2000	Jan Kopecky	2 Hr 41:51.3
2	Peugeot 207 S2000	Kris Meeke	+2:46.9
3	Peugeot 207 S2000	Nicolas Vouilloz	+2:49.5
4	Peugeot 207 S2000	Freddy Loix	+2:58.9
5	Peugeot 207 S2000	Corrado Fontana	+3:45.0
6	Skoda Fabia S2000	Alberto Hevia	+4:27.2
7	Peugeot 207 S2000	Michal Solowow	+5:58.0
8	Abarth Grande Punto S2000	Giandomenico Basso	+7:03.8

Kopecky. (SMcB)

Overall standings at end of the rally
IRC Drivers' standings

1	Kris Meeke	Peugeot 207 S2000	50 pts
2	Jan Kopecky	Skoda Fabia S2000	49 pts
3	Freddy Loix	Peugeot 207 S2000	32 pts
4	Giandomenico Basso	Abarth Grande Punto S2000	28 pts
5	Nicolas Vouilloz	Peugeot 207 S2000	25 pts

With 109 points, Peugeot retained its IRC Manufacturers' title:

IRC Manufacturers' standings

1	Peugeot	109 pts
2	Skoda	72 pts
3	Mitsubishi (Ralliart)	42 pts
4	Abarth	35 pts
5	Proton	5 pts

Hevia. (SMcB)

The sign that welcomes Kris and Paul every time they enter their service space. (SMcB)

Nagle's notes

"Asturias was a nervous rally, the pressure was on us. Skoda were starting to show their form, and Kopecky was a real threat. Jan is a fantastic competitor. After the first few stages Hevia was up in front and Jan was there or thereabouts. We were all very close, but we knew Skoda Spain were backing Hevia, and that was going to work in Jan's favour.

"We had a bit of bad luck, another wheel damaged, we had come down to a dangerous part, a 2 right, which is a slow corner, we braked about five/six feet too late, a fraction late, and fell into a drain and we broke the rim. Kris immediately said we are out of the rally, the suspension has gone, but we continued on, past the next junction, and eventually got out and found that it was only a tyre.

"I said, fuck it, fuck, fuck, fuck! We were so worried about the suspension and realised it was only a rim. I got out and changed the wheel. We changed it in about a minute and caught up to Freddy, and then got by him. That was us back in 14th. Morale was down and the pressure was on

us. Championship mode went out of the window and we went into race mode because we were so far back it didn't matter.

"Marc told us to keep pushing, keep pushing, so we got up to eighth on Friday night, and the championship was starting to play on our brains. What if Kopecky wins? Kopecky is second ... Hevia is going to lead him out, Kopecky is going to beat us, and Kopecky is going to take 10 points, and we'll maybe get one point!

"We knew Freddy was just in front of us, and that Fontana was in fifth. So that was our goal, he was a minute and a half ahead, we went as hard as the car could travel, we were flying, we got back up to fifth, then Nicola Vouillez was third. Freddy got a puncture and we leapfrogged him, and then Nico got a puncture but we were still behind him.

"With only two stages to go, Marc did not want team orders. Nicolas Vouillez has been a superb teammate and a superb champion all year, he said to Kris you are getting your third place here, I am not racing you, my championship is over.

Kris signs his autograph for the Spanish traffic cops, assisted by Melanie Kent and Marc Van Dalen. (SMcB)

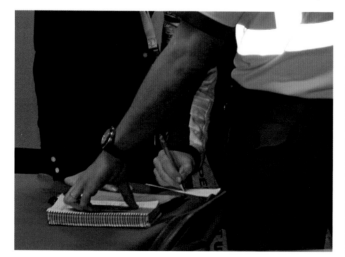

Nagle looks at his notes in service. (SMcB)

The last stage in Spain. (SMcB)

Podium celebrations. (Peugeot UK)

I want you to benefit from it. It was great credit to Nicolas, but for Kris to get back up into a position to be able to allow this, was an amazing drive, we drove to that goal, then Hevia got a puncture and this promoted us to second overall, and that meant we were leading the championship by one point going into Sanremo.

"But I said to Kris, the pressure that we were under during that rally was unbelievable.

"Nothing really clicked, the pressure mounted on us over the entire weekend, the weather was iffy, and it was a new rally and we got away with the points from second place."

Chapter 16
Champions!

Rallye Sanremo
24-26 September
IRC Round 10

Peugeot UK's Kris Meeke started the rally leading the standings, but there was now just the one point between the Peugeot UK driver and Skoda's Jan Kopecky. With Skoda winning the last two rallies, Kris' focus was on ensuring that he finished ahead of Jan when the rally came to completion.

Sanremo also saw the return to the IRC of Francois Duval, in a Fiat Abarth S2000. A total of 24 S2000 cars lined up at the start of the rally, which would be contested over a total of nine special stages, totalling 201.7km, before the finish in Sanremo town.

With just four stages on day one, you'd be excused for thinking that the drivers were going to have an easy day. No chance. The battle started in the evening, and the stages ran well into the night. The rally was fought on the famous

Kris and Marc chat – Sanremo. (Peugeot UK)

Sanremo – pitch black corner, one of many. (Peugeot UK)

Kris battles through the night stages – Sanremo. (Peugeot UK)

narrow, twisty stages of the hills and mountains above the Italian Riviera resort.

The Skoda team was up for the title fight with Kris. Kopecky went quickest on the very first stage, and opened up a two second lead over Kris who lay in third, 1.9 seconds adrift of Paolo Andreucci.

Kopecky was clearly flying, but disaster was about to strike; in the semi-darkness the Czech appeared to hit a wall and, in doing so, damaged his suspension. Kopecky was unable to repair the car and had to retire from the rally.

By Special Stage three, the darkness had set in. At only 10.62km, this was a short stage. Kris was unsure if Jan Kopecky was definitely out of the rally. If Kopecky was out, Kris could ease up if he needed to. Andreucci set the fastest time on stage three and Kris came over the finish line third fastest, 13.7 seconds off the pace.

The scene at the end of the third stage was chaotic. Reports were coming in that Kopecky was out, but I (your author) and Ian Sedgwick (Peugeot UK PR) could not get this confirmed.

Sweeping through another bend. (Peugeot UK)

Daytime stages in Sanremo. (Peugeot UK)

When Kris and Paul came through we asked had they seen anything but they were unclear of what had happened.

There was a service halt before a monster 44km stage. The organisers had made the first three stages of the rally into one epic stage, and not only was it one of the longest stages of the championship, it was also going to be run in pitch black. Kris and Paul knew their only task was to complete the SS4 safely, and this they duly did, though heavy use of the brakes brought fading in the final kilometres, and they dropped to fourth.

It was a short night's sleep for the crews, as day two began just 7 hours after day one had finished. Five stages lay between the crews and the finish ramp. All Kris had to do was finish as high up as possible, so that they could take a good lead into the final round of the series, Scotland. However, the number crunchers had worked out that if Kris and Paul finished in first place, they would take the title in Sanremo.

Starting the final day in fourth place, Kris and Paul demolished the field in the opening two stages. It was the opening stage of the day – SS5 – where the Peugeot UK crew did the initial damage, setting a time a clear ten seconds ahead of the next best driver, Italy's Renato Travalglia. Luca Rossetti took

207 as a zero car. (SMcB)

Andreucci. (SMcB)

Rossetti. (SMcB)

Vouilloz. (SMcB)

Meeke tames the mountains. (SMcB)

Flying on the Tarmac roads. (SMcB)

the lead after SS5 as overnight leader Paulo Andreucci slipped to second. Kris was flying and was up to third overall.

Stage six saw another Meeke attack. Kris again set the fastest time. He was eight seconds quicker than Travaglia on the test, taking the rally lead by 11.4 seconds ahead of Rossetti (who could only manage the sixth quickest time on the stage). Now the title was Meeke's and Nagle's for the taking.

There was to be more drama, however. Kris had been experiencing brake fade on some stages, so he decided to bleed the brakes on the Peugeot 207 S2000 before the ultra-short Stage 7, but made an error. The result – no brakes for the stage. He lost time to Luca Rossetti, and allowed the rest of the field to close the gap. Kris' lead over Rossetti was now down to 3.1 seconds. There was going to be a nail-biting end to the rally.

Hairpin bends abound. (SMcB)

The lunchtime service halt was a tense time for driver, co-driver, and the team. The media was kept at arm's length, and Kris and Paul got a little time to collect their thoughts on what had gone on.

With Jan Kopecky, their only rival for the drivers' title, already out, Kris and Paul could win the title, on this, the penultimate round of the series. But it's the oldest rule in the rally book that, to finish first, first you have to finish.

After getting their batteries recharged at service, Meeke and Nagle showed why they were the champions elect – they set the fastest time on SS8 and increased the gap by 4.5 seconds to 11.1 seconds to Rossetti, who lay in second place overall.

That left Meeke and Nagle with the title in sight, and they did not disappoint their many fans. They opted for a slight note of caution and finished the final stage third quickest, but came home to win the rally and the championship title. The celebrations afterwards, lasting long into the night, were packed with raw emotion.

Kris Meeke was overwhelmed with joy and emotion as he crossed the finish line on the final stage of the 2009 Sanremo Rally: "There's so many people I have to thank for the opportunity, I'm only one link in the chain, and there's a long

Checking the data on the laptop. (SMcB)

chain of people who helped make it happen, and without any one of them the chain would have been broken. I am just so happy, it is a dream come true."

Final times – SS9

1 Peugeot 207 S2000   Renato Travaglia
2 Peugeot 207 S2000   Freddy Loix+2.4
3 Peugeot 207 S2000   Kris Meeke+5.6
4 Peugeot 207 S2000   Nicolas Vouilloz   +5.8
5 Peugeot 207 S2000   Luca Cantamessa   +5.9
6 Abarth Grande Punto
  S2000   Luca Rossetti   +10.2

Final overall results

1 Peugeot 207 S2000   Kris Meeke
2 Abarth Grande Punto
  S2000   Luca Rossetti
3 Peugeot 207 S2000   Nicolas Vouilloz
4 Peugeot 207 S2000   Freddy Loix
5 Peugeot 207 S2000   Paulo Andreucci
6 Peugeot 207 S2000   Renato Travaglia

Drivers' Championship

1 Kris Meeke   60 points
2 Jan Kopecky   49 points
3 Freddy Loix   37 points
4 Nicolas Vouilloz   31 points
5 Giandomenico Basso   28 points

Manufacturers' Championship

1 Peugeot   112 points
2 Skoda   72 points
3 Abarth   43 points
4 Ralliart   42 points
5 Proton   5 points

Nagle's notes

"We went to Sanremo, I don't know why we were so relaxed. Well, that's the thing, as I said to Kris, if Jan wins and we do

An Italian village high in the hills above Sanremo. (SMcB)

not finish, then that is the worst thing that can happen, because then we need help in Scotland to win the championship, but if he finishes second then it doesn't matter if we finish in third.

"We had to finish better than fifth, so there was a lot of pressure on us, and there was expectations that we should be finishing in either third or fourth. Everyone was saying Italians this and Italians that, so it was a big blow to the rally when Basso went to the European championship rather than compete on the Sanremo round.

"This was a good thing for us as Basso would have been 'on it.' The first stage was good, we were close to Jan, and then on the second stage Jan clipped a wall and went out. We got a text message between two and three that Jan had lost four minutes, so then you start thinking about the championship and points and how well we have to finish.

"We got through that stage and drove terribly, we got back to service and Marc sat us down and we went through all the permutations of the championship. Kris couldn't concentrate and drove terribly.

"We were still third, and then we had to do the 44km stage in the dark, that was a long stage in the dark. 84 pages of pace notes, this is in part because Kris' notes are so in depth; for example, we would have more than 20 more pages of notes than say Nicolas Vouilloz. It was the biggest stage of the season, for a co-driver it was the hardest stage of the season, it was all corner after corner.

"So we got through, Kris lost the brakes for about four or five miles, but with maturity, age, experience, he kept off the brakes, and used the gearbox and we were really pleased that we only lost 10 seconds to Rossetti with no brakes.

"Then we got the brakes back, and that is experience, you cannot buy that. So we were only 22 seconds off the lead at the end of Friday. I would have taken 40 seconds as we were racing locals in the dark.

Powering out of a corner. (SMcB)

Neat and tidy. (SMcB)

Kris shakes Ian Sedgwick's hand – Sanremo. (Peugeot UK)

"Before we turned in, I said to Kris, sure we'll see how we get on tomorrow. Kris was up at normal at 5am to go running and landed in to me at 6am, and we went through the DVD of the recce. We do this for every rally and just went through the stages. So we went into the first stage, we did go for it. We attacked because we knew we had to push on and at least try and get Nicolas. We got to the end of the stage and every time we pass the flying finish I would say zero 7 or zero 10 or whatever time came up on my watch. I would never give him the minutes as he would know that by looking at the times as I have to give out my time card, get the road books, and put the helmets in the back.

"He said 'No, no you're wrong, it must be 27, it's a seven,' and then I started doubting myself, and he said, 'It must be 27 or 37' and I said no, there you are, it is 7. That meant we were 15 seconds quicker than anyone else, and 17 quicker than Andreucci.

"All of a sudden the bite was there, there was fire in the eyes, and we went to the next stage and it was another monster, 28km, and again we went through it on a blistering pace and we were 18 seconds quicker than anyone, and all of a sudden we were leading the rally and the championship, we turned a 14 second deficit into a 15 second lead.

"It was probably the two greatest stages that I have ever sat in a car with Kris. There were no moments, no mistakes, two clean super fast stages, it was a devastating blow to the Italians.

"On the next stage, because he is so hard on the left foot

Meeke/Nagle IRC Champions – Sanremo. (Peugeot UK)

braking, we had problems with bleeding the brakes, and we trapped air into the brakes when we put the brake fluid in. It will never happen again, all these things only happen once as you remember what you have done. The stage was only 3km, thank God, and it was all uphill, so we only dropped 10 seconds, so we led the rally by 3 seconds. We went into service and regrouped.

"We weren't stressed when we came into service, we had gone from fourth in the rally to leading it, and two stages away from the championship. The media got very uptight with us, we didn't want to do any media interviews during that final service, we didn't want the questions about tying it up here and not having to go to Scotland. We were still thinking, anything can happen, as there were 56km left and two monstrous stages

of the IRC Championship left in Sanremo. Around the service park we could feel the tension, everyone was on a knife edge, and that made us a little nervy.

"But as soon as we got back into the car, it is only me and him and the little car, and we just had a chat and said let's just do exactly the same as we had done in the morning. Not to push any harder, just go at the same pace and get the same times. It is a credit how good our notes are, 26km, 50 pages of notes and maybe 700 corners and there was only 0.6 of a difference between our first and second run through the stage.

"That is a credit to making notes and having the setup of the car right, and then we had the lead back up to 11 seconds.

"On the last stage I warned Marc to make sure that the

Meeke rolls into service as IRC Champ – Sanremo. (Peugeot UK)

Meeke/Nagle celebrate – Sanremo. (Peugeot UK)

Champagne in Sanremo. (Peugeot UK)

splits were right to the cars who were running first on the road so that we would know their times. We were 3 down and only a couple of km into the stage and we had 13 seconds of a lead, so I said to Kris, 'Keep pushing on here,' as he was backing off a bit too much. We passed the flying finish and knew we had won the rally and the championship. I cannot explain it in words, wow, it was a really emotional day, his brother was there, and our sponsors from home, and it was probably one of the greatest days ever for Irish motorsport.

"When we came into the service for the final time to get the car cleaned up for the ceremonial finish, the energy and the buzz was awesome. It was great to see the top brass from Peugeot and all the guests, it was absolutely brilliant. It was a fantastic achievement. From where we came from in Monte Carlo to Sanremo, we left Nice after Monte, I wouldn't say broken men, but the morale had taken a battering. Nobody would have

thought that nine/ten months later we would be champions. The way we worked from January to the level where we are now in Sanremo, it is all the behind the scenes stuff, like going through the onboard on the recce, going through all the notes, out running, keeping fit.

"But without Peugeot UK, without Kronos, without Peugeot Sport, none of it would have been possible. We had a faultless car, we hadn't a problem with the car. The support we have had in the UK, the support we have had from home in Ireland, has all been mega.

"Now, sitting at the Colin McRae stages, well we didn't have to come here but with the championship tied up, we were definitely coming here, I have never done this rally but I am looking forward to it, but Kris did in 2008 with his sponsors. It is a great finishing tribute. Kris doesn't have a good record on this rally, but I will do my best to keep him on the straight

Meeke/Nagle Kronos Number 1 – Sanremo. (Peugeot UK)

Sanremo podium. (Peugeot UK)

and narrow tomorrow. It is a good way to end the season, with the history between Colin and Kris. And as for Rally Scotland, there is no better place than to go there as IRC Champions, it will be a home from home.

"Scotland will be serious, and we will be going out to win it, but it will be a good party as we will have lots of support from the UK and Ireland. Many people have said to me that to see the union flag and the tricolor on the car is good for world politics. In Barum and Asturias where there are divisions, they were impressed to see both flags on the one car.

"As for me and Kris, we don't care what colour the car is, it could be pink as long as we get the results. If we hadn't had the support of Peugeot UK we would not have been here, so it is really a big thank-you to them. I am not going to thank here, there, and everywhere, you know who you are."

Sanremo trophies. (Peugeot UK)

Sanremo – winners. (Peugeot UK)

Chapter 17
Stripped of an emotional win

RAC MSA Rally of Scotland
19-21 November
IRC Round 11

The final round of the 2009 Intercontinental Rally Challenge (IRC) took place in Scotland on November 19-21st. Peugeot UK's Kris Meeke, who secured the IRC Drivers' title at the previous round in Sanremo, led off a strong gathering of local drivers in the inaugural Rally Scotland. Kris and Paul had a UK teammate for Scotland – Adam Gould would drive the BF Goodrich Drivers' Team Peugeot 207 S2000, which was also fully supported by the Kronos team.

Inaugral rally Scotland.

Rally Scotland saw Kris go head-to-head with British Rally Champion Keith Cronin, who was driving an Abarth Grande Punto S2000, Scottish Rally Champion David Bogie was in his Ralliart Lancer E9, Alister McRae lined up in a Proton Satria Neo S2000, and old sparring partner Guy Wilks was competing in a Skoda Fabia S2000 backed by Skoda UK.

Current 2009 IRC Drivers' standings

1	Kris Meeke*	Peugeot 207 S2000	60 points
2	Jan Kopecky	Skoda Fabia S2000	49 points
3	Freddy Loix	Peugeot 207 S2000	37 points
4	Nicolas Vouilloz	Peugeot 207 S2000	31 points
5	Giandomenico Basso	Abarth Grande Punto S2000	28 points

*2009 IRC Drivers' Champion

Manufacturers' standings

1	Peugeot*	112 points
2	Skoda	72 points
3	Abarth	43 points
4	Mitsubishi (Ralliart)	42 points
5	Proton	5 points

*2009 IRC Manufacturers' Champions – third consecutive year.

The first two stages of Rally Scotland were held around the grounds of Scone Palace, near Perth, the original home of the Stone of Destiny and the site of the coronations of the Kings of the Scots. The Super Special was a short blast around the

Scone Palace. (Peugeot UK)

Super Special. (Peugeot UK)

Leading rally Scotland. (Peugeot UK)

grounds, but Meeke and Nagle showed the rest of the field why they were 2009 IRC Champions, going four seconds quicker than closest rival Guy Wilks.

The 'real' stages got under way with SS3, and it was Meeke who again set the quickest time. Alister McRae in the Proton pushed really hard, and notched the second quickest time on the stage, just two seconds adrift of Kris. Guy Wilks set the third fastest time on the stage as he settled into the Fabia. This meant that Kris now had a seven second advantage over Wilks in the overall standings. The 2009 British Rally Championship winner, Keith Cronin, hit trouble and lost 45 minutes after getting stuck in a ditch.

Stage four went to Guy Wilks as he notched up his first fastest time of the rally, taking 2.9 seconds off Meeke. The Skoda driver now lay 4.1 seconds off the lead.

Sideways stuff. (Peugeot UK)

Lifting a wheel. (Peugeot UK)

Kris felt there was a problem with his left-front wheel after SS3, he explained: "I had a very strange feeling after about 5km, just on a right hander, I felt the front-left didn't have the grip that I thought it should have. I said shit, I have picked up a puncture. I said to Paul, 'We have a puncture, how far to go?' It didn't get any worse so we just kept going. I think we may have opened up the tyre too much with the cutting, and maybe the blocks got a bit worn or moved about in the middle. We also had another problem – the cable where you pull on to select reverse broke and they couldn't fix it in ten minutes at the morning service. So, if we had have spun this morning we could have been out of the rally, so we had to be extremely careful. This cable broke last night on the way into Parc Fermé."

Cleaning up. (Peugeot UK)

Mechanics at work. (Peugeot UK)

A dominant Meeke. (Peugeot UK)

No time to take in the beautiful scenery. (Peugeot UK)

On the fifth stage, Meeke was back on top of the timesheets, the newly crowned IRC Champion beat Wilks by 7.1 seconds, widening the lead to 11.2 seconds. Alister McRae in the Proton was well placed in third; 44.2 seconds off the lead.

On special stage six the two top men were trading blow for blow. Wilks notched the fastest time on this test, and slashed the deficit to just 5.6 seconds

McRae again set the third quickest time; he was losing time on the top two, but was widening his gap on those further down the order.

Meeke demonstrated his class through Craigvinean, SS7, going 15 seconds quicker than McRae and Wilks. This extended the Dungannon man's lead to 21.2 seconds over the Skoda of Wilks.

Alister McRae was driving well, and at the end of the first full day's action was in third overall; 1m 18.2 seconds off the lead.

Kris told us how he had got on: "It was very difficult because the lights were set too low and I couldn't see into the distance," he laughed. "Maybe that's why I was so quick."

More rain in a blustery Scotland. (Peugeot UK)

In the forest stages. (Peugeot UK)

Wilks was fastest on the opening stage of the final day, and regained three seconds from Meeke, but the gap was still 18.1 seconds. McRae remained in third.

Meeke replied by setting fastest times on SS9 and the monstrous 33km SS10 Loch Ard test. Kris extended the gap to Wilks, and was now leading Rally Scotland by 27.9 seconds.

Kris was really impressed with the Loch Ard stage: "That was mega, I have been lucky enough to compete on some of the best rallies in the world, and that stage ranks as one of the best in the world."

The battle continued between Meeke and Wilks on SS11, and it was the turn of the Englishman to turn the screw. Wilks in the Skoda went fastest, but it was by the slendest of margins; 0.8 of a second from Meeke.

Changing tyres before the next stage. (SMcB)

On SS12 Wilks made it two-in-a-row, and this time took a lot more off the lead; in fact, nearly seven seconds, but the word from Meeke's camp was that the 2009 IRC Champion was taking it cautiously.

The final stage of the rally was to be the repeat of the 33km of Loch Ard, but the stage was cancelled as a result of an accident involving David Bogie. Both he and his co-driver were OK, but their car blocked the road and forced the stage to be canned.

This meant that Kris Meeke won the inaugural Rally Scotland, and made it five wins in what has been a dominant display of sheer brilliance from the newly-crowned IRC Champions.

Checking the treads. (SMcB)

Meeke puts on a new front tyre. (SMcB)

Kris and the TW Steel girls. (Peugeot UK)

For Meeke, though, the victory was an emotional one. The 30-year-old spent almost three years of his early career living with Colin McRae's family in Lanark, while the former world champion funded Meeke's driving.

"This win, Rally Scotland, is for Colin," Meeke, hugged by his father Sydney said as tears welled in his eyes. "I wouldn't have been here if it hadn't been for all the help and time Colin and the McRae family gave me. To come to Scotland and to win it, it is a really emotional win, I'll have to savour this year, it has been epic."

An emotional win. (Peugeot UK)

Number 1. (Peugeot UK)

Nagle's notes

"It was a brilliant result, it was great to win in Scotland. It has been a perfect year for us, five wins and two podiums. Two seconds because of punctures, and the only blemish was Monte. Hopefully, we will come back and fix that next year. We have to get better and better, and there are going to be a lot of Skodas next year, and we do not have a teammate at the minute.

"Nicolas and Freddy do not have cars for next year, so we really need a teammate. All we can do is try our best and see what happens. There might even just be a party tonight."

Holding the trophy. (Peugeot UK)

National anthems. (Peugeot UK)

Meeke drenches McRae. (Peugeot UK)

Winners again. (Peugeot UK)

Jon Goodman MD of Peugeot UK, celebrates the win.
(Peugeot UK)

Kris and father, Sydney. (Peugeot UK)

But that would not be the end of the matter, Rally Scotland was to throw up a final sting in the tail. Five days after the finish of the 2009 Rally Scotland, Skoda UK driver Guy Wilks was declared the winner after a stewards' hearing found that the front subframe of Kris Meeke's Peugeot 207 S2000 was lighter than it should have been.

However, the authorities have claimed that there was no intention of breaking the rules on Peugeot's part, as Meeke's car was actually 20kg heavier than the Skoda when it was weighed prior to the rally start.

Peugeot Sport director Olivier Quesnel stated: "We acknowledge the stewards' decision. We're responsible for what happened, but not guilty of anything. This was down to an administrative mistake, which we intend to rectify. The mistake had no influence on the performance of the 207 Super 2000, and we must apologise to Kris Meeke, whose talent and championship title this year are beyond question."

Chapter 18
Defending the title

On a much better note, Peugeot UK confirmed that newly-crowned IRC Champions, Kris Meeke and Paul Nagle, re-signed to contest the 2010 IRC Championship.

Meeke and Nagle were delighted to be renewing their campaign, after covering 2197.73 kilometres of Special Stages and setting fastest times on 42 out of the 127 stages they completed.

Their Peugeot UK car would be run once more by the Belgium-based Kronos Racing team, which claimed two out of the last three IRC titles.

The boys were set to contest 10 out of the 12 rallies on the IRC calendar in 2010, starting off with the world-famous Monte Carlo Rally at the end of January, and were itching to emulate the success of 2009.

A very happy Kris Meeke said: "I have to say it won't get much better than this, to try and equal or surpass what we have done this year will be very hard. Next year and Monte Carlo is only around the corner. I am happy to announce that we will be trying to defend our title with Peugeot UK next year. There has been a bit of uncertainty over the last few months and everyone has been looking to know, but we have finally dotted the Is and crossed the Ts.

"For me it is impossible to go anywhere else other that Peugeot UK and Kronos. The opportunities that they have given me this year have been huge, the testing with Peugeot Sport, the collaboration with Kronos and Marc Van Dalen has been incredible. Everyone talks about the other cars getting stronger and the 207 getting older, it is still capable and Peugeot Sport has given me the commitment that they will push like hell next year to do everything they can to stay at the front, without their support it probably would have been a different decision, I am very happy to stay where I am."

Jon Goodman, Peugeot UK Managing Director was happy that Kris and Paul had signed for 2010: "It was a very easy decision to make for us to keep Kris and Paul. Marc from Kronos told us that we had to have Kris Meeke. We took Marc on trust. I don't think Marc would have signed up for so many wins. I think Kris and Paul have done a fantastic job for Peugeot the brand and Peugeot UK this year. There has been a huge amount of interest and a huge amount of dealer following. A lot of our dealers came to events to see the boys in action. It was always the idea to have a two-year programme, and there was no other pilot and co-pilot who we would be interested in working with. The difficulty for the guys is that they have set the bar very high."

Peugeot UK re-signs Kris Meeke. (Peugeot UK)

Chapter 19
The final word

"What a season, absolutely unbelievable. We started with the snow in Monte Carlo, and we finish here in Scotland in the rain on such a high. What a nice thing to do to come back to Scotland and demonstrate to the British public what Kris and Paul can do. Colin McRae, I am sure, is looking down on Kris, and he must be bloody proud of him.

"I just stand here now, it has been a great year, and watching what Paul and Kris have done is just mega. I am really proud to be part of their story. What they have done for rallying, for Peugeot UK, and for the 207 is unbelievable."

Ian Sedgwick
Peugeot UK PR Manager
Responsible for the 2009 IRC Programme

To end off a brilliant 2009, Kris Meeke was awarded 'Rookie Of The Year' at the *Autosport* Awards Ceremony.

Meeke was flying high in 2009. (Peugeot UK)

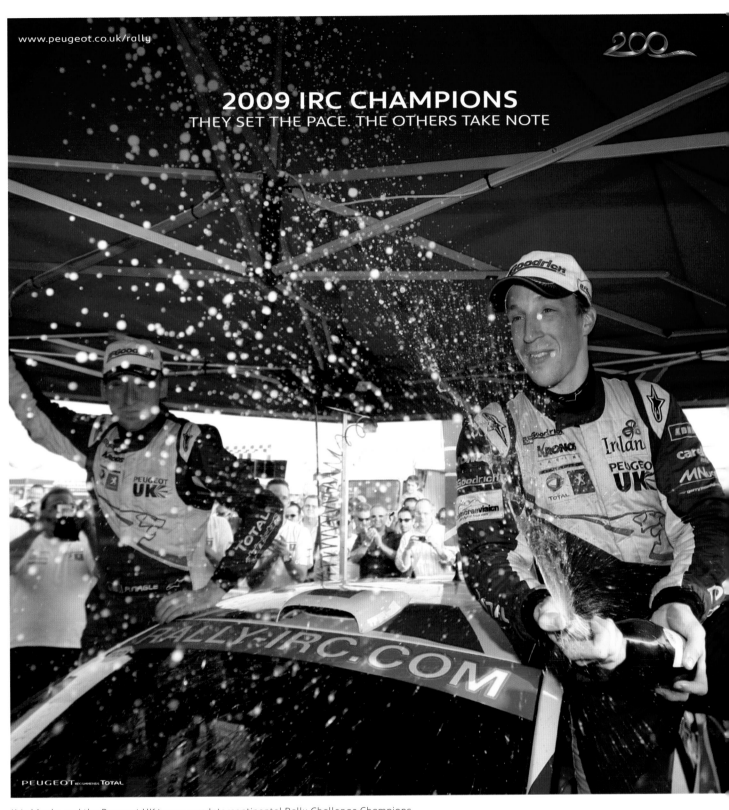

If you would like to advertise in a future reprint of this book,
please contact Veloce Publishing on (01305) 260068,
or email: jk@veloce.co.uk

Index